Ox 4/06 √ 7/07

APR 2 5 2006

ALSO BY JOSEPH ("JOE DOGS") IANNUZZI

The Mafia Cookbook Revised and Expanded

The Mafia Cookbook

Joe Dogs: The Life & Crimes of a Mobster

Cooking on the Lam

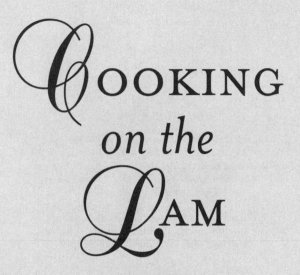

Joseph "Joe Dogs" Iannuzzi

SIMON & SCHUSTER
New York · London · Toronto · Sydney

SIMON & SCHUSTER
Rockefeller Center
1230 Avenue of the Americas
New York, NY 10020

The publisher gratefully acknowledges *The Birmingham News*
for use of the article and photo appearing February 6, 2000,
entitled "Tales from the Mob" written by Carol Roberson;
© by *The Birmingham News, 2005*. All rights reserved.
Reprinted with permission.

The stories in the book are based on real events.
In some instances, dates, names, places, and other details
were changed to accommodate my recipes.
—J.I.

For information about special discounts for bulk purchases,
please contact Simon & Schuster Special Sales at
1-800-456-6798 or business@simonandschuster.com

Designed by Helene Berinsky

Manufactured in the United States of America

10 9 8 7 6 5 4 3 2 1

Library of Congress Cataloging-in-Publication Data
Iannuzzi, Joseph.
Cooking on the lam / Joseph "Joe Dogs" Iannuzzi.
    p. cm.
1. Cookery, Italian. 2. Criminals—United States. 3. Iannuzzi, Joesph. I. Title.

TX723.I418 2005
641.5945—dc22   2005050009

ISBN-13: 978-0-7432-6980-3
ISBN-10: 0-7432-6980-2

For
Julie Hawkins
AKA Jules

Cooking on the Lam

COOKING ON THE LAM

*H*ERE I GO AGAIN, another cookbook. I have more stories to go with the recipes, also. The last time I talked to you, I was in Memphis, Tennessee. I was in the Witness Protection Program. The marshal responsible for me was Steve Popernick. I cooked for Steve a couple of times and we got along pretty good. I saw him once a month, when he came over to give me my monthly payment for my living expenses. My cost of living was as follows: Rent $650; gas and electric, about $120; telephone, $50; and then there was food, about $500 a month and gas for my car, maybe another $100. That amount came to $1,420 a month. The marshall gave me $1,252 a month.

I had to get the rest of the money somewhere, but where?

I had mentioned this to Steve, and he said get a job and then we'll adjust your allotment. We'll give you a little less until you can make enough to live on your own. I looked at him. "Get a job! Whaddya nuts! I ain't woiked in fifteen years and youse want me to go to woik now! Are you crazy! After what I did for youse guys you think I'm gonna start woiking now? Ya better figure something else out, because I ain't doin nothing. *Capito, patrone.*"

"Well, Joe Dogs, if you run out of money, you'll have to go to work if you want to eat. Your allotment is based on a single person per month. Get yourself a less expensive place to live and do a lot of walking, so you won't burn the gas in your car. There's a lot of ways you can cut down on expenses. *Capito?* I know what that word means, but I don't quite understand what the other meant," the agent remarked.

"It means like captain or like you're the boss, you know, like you're in charge." I answered.

I couldn't believe what I was hearing. I felt lost. I mean this guy is treating me like I was still with the mob. Even when he interviewed me he said a bunch of things like "Don't get in any fights. You can't call anyone in your family. Don't let anyone know who you are. Don't tell anyone where you are." And every time he mentioned something, a threat came after the phrase. "If you do that, you'll be kicked out of the program. Do you understand, Joe?" He must have said that last phrase a dozen times.

"Hey, Steve, were you ever a cop? You act just like one."

"Yes. I was in the police force for twelve years. Why?"

"Because you act just like one, that's why!" I said. "Listen, Steve, when I was interviewed, the lady told me that if I wanted my dog to be with me, to inform the marshal that I reported to and that he, meaning you, would have the authority to have my pet delivered to me. So Steven, I'm making a request for you to help me get him as soon as possible. Okay?"

"No. It's not okay. I can't do anything about your dog," Steve said. "But what I will do is take all the information down and pass it on to headquarters, and if they okay your request, then so be it," he continued.

I felt like I was in a concentration camp. This guy was tough on the federal witnesses. "All right, Steve," I said to the marshal, "but please go to headquarters as soon as possible. I miss my dog terribly and I need him with me."

J HAD BEEN in Tennessee now for about three months. Steve and I were playing golf. He had brought me my allotment for my monthly bills, which cost me almost fifteen hundred a month. Steve was an avid golfer, and he was good. We played for lunch, with automatic presses. He beat me even though he gave me strokes. It was a plush country club golf course. I wondered how he could afford a membership and a beautiful home like he has on a marshal's salary.

"Well, Joe Dogs," Steve said, laughing. "You lost three ways. You owe me breakfast, lunch, and dinner, but I'll make a deal with you."

"What?" I asked disgustedly.

"If you cook one of your Italian dishes for me, I'll call it even." Naturally I agreed, so we cleaned up at the country club and went to the supermarket. Whenever I cook a dinner, I like to do my own shopping for the groceries that I need. I got the type of veal that I wanted and the rest of the groceries. As I was about to pay for them, Steve gave his credit card to the cashier, saying to me, "We aren't allowed to accept anything from the witnesses, so although you lost the match, you're cooking. I'll have a drink and relax, while you're doing all the work. It'll be a treat to eat your cooking, so let's go to your place."

Veal Francese

4 tablespoons (½ stick) butter
½ cup flour
½ cup cornmeal
1 pound veal scaloppini, pounded thin and
  cut into 2-inch squares
1 egg beaten with a little milk
1 shallot, chopped fine
1 clove garlic, minced
Juice of ½ lemon
⅓ cup dry white wine
Salt and freshly ground black pepper

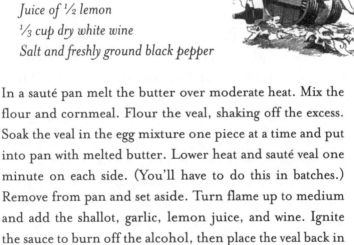

In a sauté pan melt the butter over moderate heat. Mix the flour and cornmeal. Flour the veal, shaking off the excess. Soak the veal in the egg mixture one piece at a time and put into pan with melted butter. Lower heat and sauté veal one minute on each side. (You'll have to do this in batches.) Remove from pan and set aside. Turn flame up to medium and add the shallot, garlic, lemon juice, and wine. Ignite the sauce to burn off the alcohol, then place the veal back in the pan and cook for another two minutes turning the veal over and basting it with the sauce. Season with salt and pepper to taste. Serve immediately.

Serves 4.

NOTE: Pasta marinara or Fettuccine Alfredo would go well with this dish.

$\mathcal{T}$ENNESSEE WASN'T a bad state to live in. I resided in a small town called Bartlett. Bartlett is a suburb of Memphis. For me it was a new place, new stories, and more new lies. The landlord wanted me to fill out an application with my references. The rent was $650 a month plus $650 security. It was a duplex, and it was plush. It had three bedrooms and two baths. On my side of the duplex, the backyard was enclosed with a fence. I was thinking of my pet's safety. "I won't have to worry about him getting hurt by a car or other animals," I thought to myself. I wanted it, but I figured what references I could lie about to this guy. He looks like he'd check them all anyway, so why bother. I didn't have any identification yet. We all know how swiftly the government moves. I figured I'd take a shot. Andrew was the landlord's name. "I'm a stranger to this part of the country here, sir, and to my chagrin, I lost my billfold. I went to the D.M.V. today and I'll have identification in two or three weeks. I like the place, Andrew, so I'm going to make you an offer you can't refuse," I said smiling, using one of the clichés from the *Godfather* movie.

I reached in my pocket and came out with a big roll of bills in my hand. I counted out $2,000 in front of him and his wife and handed it to him saying, "I'll give you the $650 plus $650 for the security, and I'll even pay you $650 for the last month's rent. You don't have to tell me now, Andrew. Talk it over with your wife and I'll call you in a couple of days and you can let me know what you decide. Give me a receipt for

$1,950 and $50 change from the two grand I just gave you, and I'll be on my way. Here's my phone and room number where I'm staying, in the event you want to reach me."

As I said good night and turned to walk out Andrew caught me by the car and told me that he and his wife wanted me to be their tenant, and I could move in by the first of the month. I thanked them and left. "Money talks," I said to myself.

I went out and bought new furniture. I purchased for only three rooms. The other two bedrooms I left empty. I liked it here. I'm the type of guy who minds his own business. I'm not a nosy person. But people are inquisitive. Especially if you're living in their neighborhood. They'll ask you all kinds of questions. Where you from? What made you move here? What is your occupation? And so on. I lied, naturally. The only thing is, since I got that brain damage from the mob, I kind of forget some of the lies so I had to write them down.

$\mathcal{I}$ WENT TO THE supermarket one day to do a little shopping for myself, when I noticed a lot of bundles of rapini. My mouth started to water. I bought a couple of bunches with a pound box of penne pasta. I gathered up some other groceries and went to the check-out line.

There was a man in front of me that was arguing with the cashier about the weight and price of a pound of grapes he was trying to purchase.

"Y'all owe me a dollar seventy-nine, sir," the pretty African American said to the man.

"Listen lady, I weighed the grapes myself and the scale

over there said one pound. And the sign above the grapes says $1.59 a pound. What, you trying to cheat me?"

While all this is going on, I'm saying to myself, "I had to get in this ____in' line. Couldn't I pick some other one? I mean like come on now, twenty cents, fuhgedaboudit!"

The man was getting real loud and insulting the poor girl and you could see she was about to cry. I said "Here honey, here's the twenty cents. Give the big mouth his grapes, so we all can get the hell out of here."

I didn't like the guy, especially the way he talked to the poor kid, using a couple of racial slurs. He turned to me and said, "Mind your own business. I'll pay for my own grapes," and slams me on my chest. I fell backward into the person behind me, knocking that person down. Well, before this happened I was eyeing this guy. He was about my age, I thought, about my height, and a little broader than me. My basket, with the groceries I was carrying, had fallen to the floor along with the man behind me. I helped that guy up and asked him if he was hurt. And then wheeled around and hit the loudmouth on the mouth and nose with a sucker punch. He went flying on his ass and he hit the paved floor. The manager must have called the police during the commotion because it wasn't two minutes before they arrived. A woman was screaming that I tried to kill her poor old father, who was seven years younger than me. (That, I found out later.) The cops were trying to restore order, by keeping everyone calm. The guy's daughter, whom I hadn't noticed, probably because she was nondescript, was screaming to the police "Lock him up, and beat the crap out of him." The cop in the meantime is looking over in my direction and I'm just standing there nice and quiet thinking to myself, "Now you've done it. You jerk. You were told not to get in any fights, or trouble, and look what you've done to that guy. It makes no difference that he hit you first. You antagonized him. Who's going to believe you, anyway? A mobster from New York!"

The cop came over to me, breaking me from my reverie. "Step over here, sir, please. What is your name?" After I answered all his questions he went over to the cashier who was shaken up from the ordeal, and was telling the police officer what she saw and heard. The cop came back to me and said, "The cashier backs your story to the hilt. Where you from, Joe? You're not from here, not with that accent. You sound like my dad. We're from Jersey."

"A break," I thought. "I'm from New York," I said.

"What brings you to these parts of the country? Are you with the program?"

"Smart," I guessed. I should have told him no, but he seemed like a regular guy, so I said "You clocked it, Bill, and if the marshal finds out about this my head is on the block. In fact if he finds out that I told you about me being in the program, it'll be the same result."

"I'm not taking you in, don't worry—if anything I'll lock that guy up. Where's his bigmouth daughter? I'm going to tell her to bring her old man in as soon as he gets out of the hospital, and that you're pressing charges against him because he hit you first and you have witnesses. You know what you should do, Joe, take your groceries home, then come to the station and file a complaint to cover yourself. I'll talk to my sarge; we'll take care of everything, Joseph!" Bill said with a smile.

I did what Bill had requested and then I went home and made the dish I was yearning for.

Tuscan Bean Crostini

1 (14-ounce) can cannellini beans, drained and rinsed
Extra-virgin olive oil
Freshly ground black pepper
Mediterranean sea salt
Small bunch of fresh basil leaves, torn into pieces
6 to 8 fresh oregano leaves, torn into small pieces
1 crusty baguette
3 cloves garlic, crushed

Place the drained, rinsed beans in a small bowl and pour in a small amount of the olive oil (approximately ¼ cup). Season with the pepper and sea salt. Add the basil and oregano and refrigerate for 1 to 2 hours allowing the beans to marinate in the olive oil.

Slice the baguette thinly on an angle. Place the crostini on a baking sheet. Blend together the fresh crushed garlic with ½ cup of olive oil in a small bowl. Brush the olive oil mixture onto the crostini and bake in a preheated 450-

degree oven until nicely browned. Turn bread over, brush again, and bake until toasted.

Cool the crostini and spread the bean mixture onto the bread. If desired, you may drizzle some additional olive oil on the individual appetizers. Serve with a nice bottle of pinot grigio.

Makes about 24 crostini.

Broccoli Rabe (aka Rapini)

2 bunches of rapini, cleaned and stems removed
½ cup extra-virgin olive oil
4 cloves garlic, crushed
1 pound penne pasta
Freshly grated Romano cheese
Crushed red pepper

Blanch rapini in salted boiling water for about five minutes. Remove from the heat and drain. Reserve the water (this is an important step). Bring the water back to a boil.

Warm the olive oil in a sauté pan, and sauté the garlic over low heat. Do not burn! Add the broccoli rabe and cook until tender.

Meanwhile cook the pasta in the reserved water to

al dente. Drain the pasta and add it to the broccoli and olive oil mixture. Toss to mix well.

Serve hot with Romano cheese and crushed red pepper.

Serves 4.

NOTE: This is a dish the peasants in Sicily ate. It is not only delicious but very healthy also.

BILL, MY COP PAL, told me the guy that I hit came to the station and did not file a complaint. "We told him we'd talk to you and that we'd try to convince you to drop the charges." Bill invited me to his home where he lived with his fiancée. Sheila had two children: Ben, who was about six years old, and Candice. Candice was three or four years of age at that time. The children were beautiful like their mother, and Bill and Sheila complemented one another whenever they were together. They were a good-looking family.

Sheila invited me over for a chicken dinner that Sunday. I had become good friends with them. She told me that her mother was married to an Italian man, and that her mother gave her this recipe. She wanted my honest opinion of the taste. I went to dinner, had a wonderful time, and a delicious meal. I asked Sheila for the recipe.

Chicken à la Andrea

3 tablespoons extra-virgin olive oil
3 tablespoons butter
4 boneless and skinless chicken breasts
Salt and freshly ground black pepper
4 to 6 slices thinly sliced proscuitto, cut into small pieces
1 clove garlic minced
1 cup dry white wine
4 or 5 ripe tomatoes, peeled and chopped fine
Chicken stock
1 to 2 tablespoon fresh oregano leaves, torn into small pieces

Put the olive oil and butter in a large sauté pan, over moderate heat. Season the chicken on both sides with salt and pepper. When the butter is melted and hot, put in the chicken breast pieces and cook for 3 minutes on each side over a low flame. Add the proscuitto and garlic and cook 2 minutes more, moving the chicken around. Pour the wine over the chicken. Cover the pan with a lid and simmer 3 minutes. Add the tomatoes, salt and pepper to taste, cover with a tight lid, and simmer 20 minutes. (Add a little chicken stock if it looks dry.) Sprinkle oregano over the top of the chicken 5 minutes before removing from the heat.

Serves 4.

NOTE: Any kind of pasta would complement this dish. Follow the cooking instructions on the package.

$\mathcal{I}$ WAS STARTING to put on a little weight, so I started to exercise a little. Every morning I'd force myself to walk a mile. At night I got enough exercise tearing up the losing dog track tickets. I wasn't supposed to go to the racetrack, or anywhere that there was gambling. It was too dangerous for me. The mob was still looking for me.

I missed my dog terribly. Steve never told me anything about whether or not he got the okay to get the animal. I mean like come on, it's been almost five months now since him and I talked about the dog. "Screw him," I said to myself. I'll get my dog on my own. He never comes around here, anyway. When he brings my allotment over, he calls first, then drives over to my place and blows the horn. I go out, and get the money while he's in the car.

"Hello, Mom, it's me—your pride and joy. Mom! Do me a favor? Get a pen and paper, and write this down." I gave her my address and asked her to put my dog on a plane to Memphis the next day. I had to have him. I was tired of calling my mother every day to talk to my dog. My mother would put the phone to the dog's ear and I would say, "Daddy loves you, Giuseppe." (Giuseppe means Joe in Italian.) "I miss you, baby boy," I'd continue. I mean, like I did this almost every day. My phone bills were over a hundred a month just talking to my dog. When I went out to eat on a date, if we had steak, I'd ask the waiter for my steak bone. I'd take it home and wrap it with plastic wrap and then tin foil and FedEx it to my mother for my dog. That's really sick. The best was, I knew he liked to chew on a ham bone. I went out and bought a ham hock, baked it and trimmed a lot of the meat off of it, then shipped it FedEx. "Now, come on. That ain't normal," I murmured to myself.

I went to the airport and picked up my Yorkie. He was so happy to see me he barked at me for an hour. Scolding me for not getting him sooner, I assumed. Now I was in my glory. "Screw the marshals, their organization and even Clinton, if he's involved with their outfit."

*I*N MEMPHIS I met a very pretty woman who worked at the dog track as a teller. She used to come over for lunch once in awhile. This one particular day I made a nice Northern Italian lunch for us.

Fettuccine Alfredo

8 tablespoons (1 stick) butter
1 pint half & half
Freshly ground black pepper
½ cup freshly grated Romano cheese
1 pound fettuccine pasta, cooked al dente
4 egg yolks
Salt

In a large stainless-steel frying pan, melt the butter over low to medium heat. Once the butter is melted, pour in the half & half and bring to a boil. Add the cheese and stir. Grind some black pepper in at this point. Put the pasta in the sauce and toss slightly. Place the egg yolks on the top of the pasta and toss repeatedly until the sauce gets a smooth blended texture. Add more pepper and salt to taste. Serve hot immediately.

Serves 2 to 4.

I WAS IN MEMPHIS for a year now and Steve never saw the dog, yet. That's how close the marshals watch over you. Then again I never saw the marshal anyway. Only on pay day.

Steve was due to come and bring my allotment today. He called first and then drove over and leaned on the horn.

I in turn went outside and got the dough. "How's everything going?" Steve asked me.

"Great," I answered.

"Did you get a job yet? You know the government wants you to be able to help support yourself."

"Well, I was looking into a position and I was told I'd be accepted with a diploma, as there is some schooling involved. Would you people, by you people, I mean your organization, send me to school? What I mean is pay for my tuition?"

"I'm almost definite they would, as we encourage the witnesses to try and get educated and support themselves," Steve said.

"That's great," I said. "I'll check on the enrollment dates and see how much dough you need to get in."

"What type of school are you going to go to? What's the trade?"

"I'm going to become a brain surgeon. It's extensive training—probably six years of schooling, and I'd have to be shipped out of state to California, or Seattle, Washington." As I continued talking, Steve didn't respond—he just drove away slowly while my conversation with him was only half finished. "That was rude," I thought. "The *faccia merda.*"

I went in and told my pal Giuseppe I didn't think we were going to the brain surgeon school. He looked pissed off and barked. I called my friend Karen over for some dessert and coffee.

Sheryl's Amaretto Cheese Tart

1 uncooked prepared piecrust
One 8-ounce package cream cheese
1/2 cup sugar
3/4 cup amaretto
Strawberries, sliced
Kiwi, peeled and sliced
Blueberries
Raspberries
Apricot preserves

Press down the piecrust in a tart pan. Poke holes in it with a fork. Bake the pie shell in a preheated 325-degree oven until golden brown. Remove from the oven when done, and let cool. Leave the crust in the pan.

In a small bowl, beat the cream cheese until smooth. Add the sugar and continue to mix until dissolved. Add half the amaretto; reserve the other half for the glaze. Spread the cream cheese mixture over the cooled crust. Arrange the sliced fruit on top of the tart, and add the berries in between the fruit slices. Heat the remaining amaretto and apricot preserves until melted and spread on the cheese tart to glaze the fruit. Refrigerate until ready to serve.

Serves 6 to 8.

"THAT TART WAS GREAT! Where did you learn how to make that?" Karen asked.

"My daughter, Sheryl, who lives in Florida, gave it to me. She's a great cook. You've got to meet her, Karen. She's beautiful. Let's go to the movies. There's a good Mafia picture playing. Whaddya say?"

"Okay, Joe! You act just like those Mafia guys. Did you ever kill anyone?" She asked. I smiled at Karen before I answered. She was such a beautiful lady.

"I know I hurt someone's feeling's once," I said to her, still smiling. She was a married woman with two children. We were friends; we had a platonic relationship. Karen would come over and clean my apartment whenever I called her. She needed the extra cash. I didn't mind helping her out that way at all.

She cleaned my apartment with gusto and she was immaculate. I liked her very much.

I WAS IN TENNESSEE for about eighteen months and I was starting to get used to it. I was relaxing in the living room watching television when I heard this crash from my dining room. I grabbed my .38 revolver, which was always close by. I rushed into the dining room to find the plate glass window broken. I noticed a big rock with a white piece of paper wrapped around it, with a thick rubber band to hold the note. I removed the paper from the rock and read what was written there. It said, "We don't want your kind around here! So you best leave the area, or we'll do something to make your stay here miserable, and you'll be sorry for not listening to us." The note was in all print. I dialed the number Steve gave me to reach him in the event I needed to. All the time I had been in this area, I never used the number. I got his voice mail with an emergency number if needed or leave a message. I thought it over for a couple of minutes and decided that it wasn't life threatening, so I dialed his number again and left a message of what happened. I also asked that he get in touch with me as soon as possible because I was worried that they might do something to my Yorkie.

Steve came over the next afternoon and questioned me and asked me if I touched the rock and the note. I told him I did, as I had to so that I could read it. He picked up the rock with a handkerchief and the note with tweezers, and looked at me and said, "This is the way you should have handled both items. That way we could get the prints off of them, without finding yours on the evidence."

"I'm sorry, Steve," I said, "but I didn't take that 007 training." I was telling Giuseppe not to bother Steve as he was doing his thing with the evidence. "You know, Steve, I think whoever threw that rock must have recognized me from that A&E tape." A&E had filmed me in a documentary before I went in the program.

The marshal didn't answer me. Instead he asked, "How and when did you get your dog here? You know you weren't supposed to be in touch with anyone in your family. I'm going to have to make a report and send it to headquarters."

"Hey, Steve, that's not the Yorkie I had. He's still with my mother. I got this dog last week."

"Well he looks just like the dog in the picture you showed me, and he has the same name and . . ."

I cut him short. "Yo Steve! All Yorkies look alike! And as for his name, I named him Giuseppe. Why can't there be more than one dog with the same name? Besides he's comfortable with that name. What about you? Your name is Steve. Do you have a monopoly on that name? Can't anyone else use your name? Come on, Steve! You are talking like a man with a paper ass! Go ahead! Write your report. I'll make you look like a jerk. Can you imagine what all the animal lovers would say about this?" Steve was quiet. While he was doing his investigative work I was cooking for us.

Filet Mignon Oscar

2 prime filet mignons, 6 to 8 ounces each
10 asparagus spears
1 (8-ounce) can lump crab meat
1 (10-ounce) bag fresh spinach, stems off, rinsed but not dried
1 cup hollandaise sauce (recipe follows)

Cook the steaks in the broiler or outdoor grill.

While the steaks are cooking, open the crab meat and microwave it on a dish for fifteen seconds to take the chill out; set aside. Steam the spinach; set aside. Microwave the asparagus. While the steaks are cooking and the asparagus is in the microwave, start your hollandaise sauce. When the steaks are done, place them in a dish and keep them warm in a preheated 225-degree oven.

HOLLANDAISE SAUCE

3 jumbo egg yolks
8 tablespoons (1 stick) butter, melted
Juice of ½ lemon
¼ teaspoon dry mustard
2 tablespoons dry white wine
Salt and ground white pepper

Place egg yolks, lemon juice, mustard, and wine in a stainless-steel bowl. Have a larger bowl ready with ice water. Place the stainless-steel bowl on top of a pot filled halfway with simmering water. This is now a double boiler. Start by whisking the egg mixture for about two minutes, then pour in the butter in a slow, thin stream, still whisking all the while (otherwise you'll have scrambled eggs). Continue this procedure until you have a sauce with the right consistency. Float the stainless-steel bowl on the bowl with the ice water to stop the cooking. Keep stirring for at least another minute. Season with salt and pepper.

Put the warm steaks on two plates, and apply a layer of warm crab meat, then a layer of steamed spinach. Spoon the hollandaise sauce over the top, using all the sauce divided evenly, and finally arrange the asparagus over the top.

Serves 2.

NOTE: This particular dish can be found in your finer restaurants.

STEVE AND I were playing golf at the country club where he was a member. We were on the back nine when his cell phone started ringing. I was walking toward the green when I over-heard my name in his conversation. I waited for him by the green. I expected Steve to say something to me, but instead he was lining up his golf ball getting ready to putt. "What was the phone call about? I heard you mention my name," I asked, getting a little irritated, knowing it had something to do with me. Steve was still staring at the hole and lining his putter in which direction to hit the ball. "I'll tell you as soon as I putt."

Steve retrieved his ball from the hole, turned facing me and said, "Your dad passed away last night." Then he continued to practice his putting stroke.

I was in a little bit of a shock. Well, not really, but I was concerned. I mean I loved my father, I guess! I really didn't know. But, hey, a death in your family isn't the nicest thing you want to hear.

"Steve, I'd like to go to my dad's wake. I'm going to need security and a round trip ticket." He didn't answer me. He continued his practicing with the putter.

"Steve! Did you hear what I said? I said that . . ."

He cut me off. "I heard what you said. I was just thinking, Joe! It's not up to me. It's up to headquarters. I've told you that time and time again," Steve said, getting a little annoyed. "Let's stop playing today. I'll have to get on the phone and make all the necessary arrangements, if they allow you to go with security." We left the course with Steve telling me that he'd be in touch in an hour, no longer than two.

I went home and waited. It wasn't long the phone started to ring. It was the marshal telling me that headquarters declined the trip to my father's wake and/or funeral, because it was too dangerous for me and the marshals involved, especially since the rock-throwing incident at my apartment.

"My boss told me to tell you that if you go to your father's wake in New Jersey, you'll no longer be under the protection of the government. You will be on your own. We will discharge you from the program."

"So when are they going to move me? I mean if it's so dangerous here, what the ____ am I still doing here? I thought you guys were a protection agency. I think you're all full of crap."

"Well, Joe, I'm sorry you feel that way. We are doing it for your own protection. Stay home. Don't do anything foolish." He hung up.

I lay around for a while and then I asked my neighbor if she'd like to accompany me for a nice salad and a few drinks. She agreed to the invitation. When I told her we would have dessert also, she responded, "Real dessert?"

"Yeah, both if you want," I said.

Insalata con Genoa

2 large tomatoes, cut in bite-size pieces
1 small cucumber, peeled and sliced thin
A handful of fresh basil leaves, torn
1 small red Spanish onion, sliced paper thin
1 bunch of scallions, trimmed and sliced
1 clove garlic, minced
¼ pound salami, cut in small chunks
¼ pound imported provolone cheese, cut in small pieces
1 cup pitted black olives (more if you like)
1¼ cups extra-virgin olive oil
2 tablespoons red wine vinegar
3 to 4 tablespoons balsamic vinegar
Salt and freshly ground black pepper
1 tablespoon dried oregano

In a large wooden salad bowl, combine the tomatoes, cucumber, basil, onion, scallions, garlic, salami chunks, provolone, and olives. Sprinkle the olive oil over the salad. Add the vinegars, season with salt and pepper to taste, and then toss salad thoroughly. Refrigerate for one hour. Add the oregano and toss again, adjusting seasoning as you go along. Serve immediately.

Serves 2 as a meal, 4 as an appetizer.

Bread Pudding with Whiskey Sauce

2 or 3 slices each white bread, whole wheat, and pumpernickel,
*   torn into small pieces*
3/4 cup white raisins
1 large apple, peeled, cored, and cut into bite-size pieces
1 cup (2 sticks) butter, melted
3 cups milk
6 jumbo eggs
1 tablespoon vanilla
1 cup sugar
1 to 2 tablespoons cold butter, diced

In a 9 x 9 x 3-inch baking dish, place one third of the bread; sprinkle one-half the raisins over the bread. Then put a layer of half the apple. Repeat this process one more time,

and end with the bread on top. Pour the melted butter over
the bread. Heat the milk until almost boiling. Beat the eggs
well with the vanilla and sugar. Add the egg mixture to the
hot milk, stirring rapidly, and then pour over the bread.
Dot the top with the cold the butter. Set it in a larger pan or
oven dish with an inch of water and bake at 375 degrees for
40 to 45 minutes.

Serves 6 to 8.

WHISKEY SAUCE

1 pint heavy cream
8 tablespoons (1 stick) butter, melted
½ pound confectioners' sugar (about 2 cups)
1½ ounces whiskey of your choice

Mix all together with a whisk until it all blends into a smooth
sauce. Refrigerate until ready to serve. Pour the cold sauce
over warm pudding.

Makes about 3 cups.

It WAS APRIL, 1993. I had my first cookbook published. My
publicist, Holly Zappala, had made all the arrangements for
me to appear on the David Letterman show. It was going to
be a great opportunity for my cookbook to do well. I was very
happy. Now I'd have to get permission from the marshals, as

I really needed their security for this trip. I still didn't hear anything about moving. It was the time of the month to get paid so I expected a call from Steve.

The marshal blew the horn for me to come out. I went outdoors and motioned for him to come in because "I've got something important to discuss with you." When he was inside I said "Listen, I have a chance to go on David Letterman's show. I'll need some security when I go."

"I'd like some help with this. Tell headquarters that Simon & Schuster is paying for my flight." Based on the negative responses I'd gotten in the past, I wasn't optimistic. I mean, they wouldn't even let me go to my father's funeral!

"You know we are going to move you, don't you?" Steve said.

"Yeah, I know, but when?" Steve said he would let me know when he heard from headquarters.

I called my friend Karen and asked her to come over to clean my apartment, and I would make her some lunch. She agreed and said, "I'll be there in an hour." So I started to prepare.

Orecchiette di Pollo

½ pound orecchiette pasta
1 bunch of broccoli, florets only
2 cloves roasted garlic, skinned and mashed
4 to 5 tablespoons diced sun-dried tomatoes
¼ cup extra-virgin olive oil, plus extra for the pasta
¼ cup dry white wine
2 boneless and skinless chicken breasts, cut into strips
1 teaspoon crushed red pepper
½ cup chicken stock
Freshly grated pecorino cheese

Cook the pasta al dente. While the pasta is cooking steam the broccoli and set aside. Sauté the garlic and sun-dried tomatoes lightly in the olive oil; add the wine, chicken strips, and red pepper. Add half the chicken stock and cover with a tight lid. Simmer for 10 to 15 minutes, adding more chicken stock if needed.

After the pasta is done, drain off all the water and pour a couple of ounces of olive oil over the pasta; stir vigorously. This prevents the pasta from sticking. When the sauce is done, add the broccoli and pasta to the pan. Toss over the heat to mix. Add pecorino cheese to taste, toss again, and serve.

Serves 2.

$\mathcal{I}$ WAS SCHEDULED to be in New York Thursday so I figured I'd better make my own plans for security with Simon & Schuster since headquarters wasn't going to help me out. My F.B.I. Agent friend Chris was picking me up at the airport, so I made all the arrangements to meet the guard at the Ramada Inn. The F.B.I. office was in the same building. After I got off the plane, Chris and I along with a couple of friends and an actress went out for dinner. The food was fantastic. I told Chris there would be eight tickets for him at the pick-up window, and to take whoever he wanted to the show. After dinner I went to the prepaid hotel room and met the security guard, whose name was Jim. We had adjoining rooms. Mine had a kitchenette in it, so I gave Jim some cash and a list of what groceries I needed to cook breakfast. Jim left and went to an all-night supermarket to buy the groceries. I watched a little TV and after Jim came back, he checked on me and said good night. I felt a little secure so I fell off to sleep instantly.

I woke up around 8 A.M. Took a shower, shaved, and I started the coffee. Jim had stuck his head in to see that everything was kosher, and I told him to come in and have a cup of coffee, while I prepared breakfast.

Fresh Asparagus Frittata

1 pound asparagus, trimmed: use tips only
5 to 7 jumbo eggs
Sea salt and freshly ground black pepper
2 tablespoons extra-virgin olive oil
2 tablespoons butter
½ cup drained, diced roasted peppers
½ cup diced pecorino cheese

Blanche the asparagus 1 to 2 minutes in boiling water. Drain and place in a bowl of ice water. Remove, pat dry, and set aside.

In a large bowl, beat the eggs and add salt and pepper to taste. Put the olive oil and butter in an ovenproof skillet over low heat. Cut the asparagus into quarters and sauté them with the peppers about 5 minutes. Pour in the beaten eggs and stir lightly with a rubber spatula. Cook over low heat until set on the bottom. Add the pecorino, and cook until the cheese starts to melt. Remove the skillet from the heat and place in a preheated 325-degree oven. Bake until slightly brown and the eggs are firm. Let stand for 10 minutes, and then cut into wedges. Serve warm.

Serves 2 to 4.

THE SECURITY GUARD and I took a cab to the Letterman show. We got there on time at 11 A.M., and went straight to the green room. That's where all the guests wait before they go on the stage. I was so excited that I had to go to the men's room. David Letterman to me was the best. I really wanted to meet him in person, and to be on his show was a dream come true. I was looking forward to pounding veal with David, and making him a dish that he would hunger for at another time. He was sort of like my idol in TV.

After I returned from the bathroom, a tall, good-looking young man and an extremely attractive lady approached me. He introduced himself as Dan Kellison and his secretary Lisa, whom I had spoken with many times over the phone. "Mr. Iannuzzi, I'm embarrassed and sorry to say that we have to use someone else in your place. David will not do the show with you on the stage. I know you probably went to a lot of trouble to get here, but there is nothing I can do. It's out of my hands," he said. "I'm sure you'll understand."

I was silent, I don't know for how long. I was thinking. I mean, you can't blame this guy. You really can't blame Letterman either. I wouldn't want to go on the stage with me, wondering and worrying, if someone is going to shoot at you.

I was separated from my reverie when Lisa said, "Mr. Iannuzzi, Mr. Iannuzzi, are you all right?"

I looked at Kellison and said, "Listen to me, Danny boy! You promised me that I wouldn't get bounced. Do you remember that? Answer me, you ____. Do you remember that statement?" I started to get tough. I figured, let them call the cops, I didn't care. I'd make a big thing out of it. I didn't care anymore. I was so disappointed. I was hurt. Of course there was nothing I could do, but I was going to make them sweat a little.

"Of course I remember, Mr. Iannuzzi, but there's nothing that I could possibly do. I wish this didn't happen. It's not my fault. David refuses to appear with you."

"Oh yeah," I said, continuing my charade. "Well, you get David on the phone right now. You tell that son of a _____ to come here now." This kid was terrified. I was winking at the guard so he knew I was fooling around.

"Lisa, please call security! Now! Call now, please."

"There's no need for that, Dan. Why don't you call David as Mr. Iannuzzi asked you to and let David tell Mr. Iannuzzi the reason why he won't appear with him. Please, Mr. Iannuzzi," Lisa said, looking at me. "Let's see if we can take care of this issue amicably."

"Sure, Lisa, I don't want any problems, I just want to tell that SOB what trouble and expense I went to to get here, and you can't blame me."

Dan grabbed the phone and started dialing. I grabbed the phone from his hands as soon as he was finished, and I heard it ringing. "Hello," a voice on the other end of the receiver said.

"David?" I said.

"Yes, who's calling?" he responded.

"It's Mr. Iannuzzi—Joe Dogs!" As soon as I mentioned my name, he hung up the phone. I didn't do or say anything for about ten seconds. The people in the room didn't know David had hung up on me, so I continued to act like a telephone tough guy calling him names and telling him I was going to kick his ass all over Manhattan. Then I hung up the phone.

A minute later the phone starts ringing. I thought it was Letterman, but it was Holly Zappala, my publicist. She was supposed to be there but the car she hired for the trip was involved in an accident. She called to say she would be a little late. Kellison explained the problem to her and he told her how annoyed I was and everyone here was intimidated by me. She must have asked to speak to me because Dan handed me the phone.

"Yeah, Holly, what's up?"

"Joe! Stop screwing around! Stop scaring those nice people. I'll be there in fifteen minutes! Behave!"

I smiled.

Holly came and we said our goodbyes. I told the producer Dan that I was only fooling around. We shook hands and, smiling, he said, "Lisa told me that when she called you were a real ball buster." We left and went to Brooklyn for a nice lunch.

The newspapers got wind of what happened and I gave them an interview. The interview hit almost all of the newspapers in the country, which was a good advertisement for my cookbook.

IT WAS MY SECOND DAY back in Memphis. The marshal called me and said he had to see me tomorrow. I asked what it entailed.

"Are you guys finally going to move me?" And he answered "I'll tell you tomorrow. Just make sure you're available. I'll be at your place between ten and noon tomorrow."

I immediately started to pack my clothes. I drove to the corner liquor store and got a few boxes to pack my dishes, pots and pans, etc. I was wondering where in God's name they were going to move me. I guess it really didn't make any difference. I'm sure they wanted me safe somewhere, or so I thought.

After packing I felt like having a snack. I had met this beautiful Latina nurse at Southland Dog Track a few weeks ago, and we hit it off pretty well. Her name was Lillian. She preferred to be called Lilly. After the races we went out to have a couple of drinks at this New York–style club I used to frequent occasionally. It was while we were dancing that she told me about this recipe that her dad had given her. "Try it and I'm sure you'll love it, Gringo!" Lilly said, smiling. (Lilly had given me the pet name "Gringo.") She was a traveling nurse, and I thought to myself "Gee, she's so nice. Also very pretty. I wish she lived around here. Just my luck she'll be leaving next week!" I saw her another time before she left. She gave me her cell phone number and I still have it to this day.

Mario's Mexican Shrimp Cocktail

1 (1-pound) bag frozen cocktail shrimp
1 (12-ounce) bottle seafood cocktail sauce (Heinz preferred)
1/4 cup minced sweet onion
2 tablespoons freshly squeezed lime juice
1 tablespoon minced cilantro
Dash of Louisiana hot sauce or your favorite brand
1 avocado, peeled and cut into small pieces

In a bowl, put the frozen shrimp with all the ingredients except the avocado. When the shrimp have thawed out, add the avocado and mix gently with a rubber spatula.

Serves 4 to 6.

So THIS IS the Mexican-style shrimp cocktail. I like it. I'll bet that pretty baby doll Lilly is a hot tamale herself. "The cocktail had a great flavor to it, and the avocado complemented the shrimp sauce," I mumbled to myself.

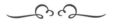

THE MARSHAL called at 11:30, and said he would be right over. When he arrived he got right down to telling me what was on his mind.

"Well, Joe," he started. "You're no longer in the program. You're on your own. Headquarters found out about your trip to New York and, by you going up there, you violated the rules that I've been preaching to you ever since you arrived here. You should have never gone to New York. You knew you weren't supposed to go there. Did you think we wouldn't find out?"

"Hold off there, Stevie Boy! I told you a month ago that I wanted to go to New York. You people are supposed to move me anyway. Are you overlooking your responsibility on that matter? The marshals' service has done everything in its power to get rid of me and now they've found an excuse."

"I'm sorry you feel that way, Joe. I have my orders, and I'm carrying them out."

"Listen, Steve. If you guys want to throw me out of the program, do it the right way. You knew that I've been recognized here. You were supposed to move me two months ago, and you didn't. Are you waiting for me to get killed? Let me tell you something, sonny! I helped the Feds put two Mafia families out of business. I put my life on the chopping block every day for over two years, so if you think I'm just gonna leave, like a quiet little lamb, you're wacky. You go tell those empty suits that you're working for that I'm not being cooperative with you, and that I plan to make a lot of trouble for your lousy organization. I have a reporter friend at the *Washington Post* and he will listen to me as to what I've learned about how you guys operate. It might put the wiseguys back on the streets, if I spread some of my knowledge to the *Post*," I said.

"Well, Joe, you're just aggravated now. You'll get over it. I suggest you leave the area as soon as you can, as it might be dangerous for you," Steve said.

"All right, Steve," I said, "you have to make me do this the hard way. Now please leave because I have a lot of thinking to do. Are you going to give me any money to move and to get relocated?"

"No, Joe! We've given you all we are going to give you! As I said before you're on your own. You no longer have the protection or services of our program. Remember you're on your own," he said, walking out the door.

I immediately called an F.B.I. agent who was still good friends with me. They all were still my friends, but this one had warned me about the marshal system, and how they worked. "They look for things that they can pick on. The witnesses who don't testify any longer are the ones the marshals' service is happy to boot out of the program," the agent had said.

The agent gave me the names and phone numbers of a few bigwigs who were working in the program in Washington, DC. I started calling them and telling everything that I was going to tell the newspapers. I was a big pest to them, so to speak, and I wouldn't let up for one minute. My mother (may she rest in peace) was aware of my problem and she wrote a congressman. I continued to hound them exhaustively every single day from 9 A.M. to 5 P.M., Monday to Friday, every hour on the hour, for three weeks. I called my reporter friend and he made a call to someone in the program, and the next day Marshal Steve Popernick came to my place of residence and said, "Joe, my boss is pissed off. I don't know what you did to make him that way but you did something."

"Oh, what a ____in' shame," I answered.

"I have two checks for you, and after I give them to you I suggest you leave the area as soon as possible. One check is for $3,500 to get you relocated, and the other is for $7,500, six months' allotment to help you get started at your new location." As Steve was leaving he said, "Don't forget you're on your own now, so be careful. Whatever you think of me is your own business, but it was my job to tell you what I did, and I never meant any harm to you. Take care of yourself and good luck to you." Steve was a good guy just doing his job.

$\mathcal{I}$ MOVED TO Charlotte, North Carolina, two weeks later with all my furniture. Charlotte was a nice city, with pretty nice clubs and restaurants, but no action. Oh, I'm sure there had to be something illegal going on, but me being an outsider I would never be able to find out. I had a real hard time renting a decent place. I couldn't give any references, as I never could leave a forwarding address. That was too dangerous. After all I did for the government, it was a shame how they treated me. I was becoming immune to adversity.

I looked in the Charlotte newspaper and saw an advertisement for apartment rentals with a six-month lease. I called the telephone number of the rental and spoke with the manager and got the address. I went through the procedure of filling out the application with a bunch of lies and gave her $35 for a credit check fee. The manager said that this was a normal procedure, paying for a reference and credit check application. There seemed to be a problem.

"Look, lady, I'm giving you fourteen hundred cash. I'll sign a six-month lease and, believe me, you won't have to worry about anything. I'm a freelance writer. I gave you thirty-five bucks to check my credit and you even said nothing bad came up, so either rent me the apartment, or give me the money I gave you back to me." What a ripoff that credit check payment is.

"I'm terribly sorry, sir. If you read the receipt that you signed, it says in small print if your credit check comes back unfavorable your money isn't refundable."

"But, Alice darling, you yourself said my credit wasn't bad, so why don't you take a shot and lease the apartment to me for six months and I'll be the best tenant you ever had. Let's go have lunch, and you think about it. My treat?" This was the way I had to conduct myself, whenever I had to rent a new place in a new city and state. Cons, lies, and charisma. I had no credit or apartment references that I could show or put on an application, that's how much help the so-called marshals' service gave you. None!

Alice agreed to have lunch with me and, at lunch, she explained what she did with 90 percent of the people who tried to rent apartments.

"The owner turns down no less than twenty applicants a day, sometimes more. There's always something that comes up so that we keep the cash and don't rent. Look at all the money he makes and I'm the one who has to turn them down. You can force us to rent to you, because your credit check came up clean. In fact, I can't find out anything about you.

"So there you have it. The apartment is yours."

I thanked her and invited her for dinner as soon as I was settled in. I told her of my cooking abilities and she suggested that I go with her to the grocery store and shop to cook at her place of residence. I agreed and found that Alice loved fish. I cooked a red snapper Italian-style.

Fillet of Red Snapper Italian-Style

Extra-virgin olive oil
1 tablespoon Butter
1 (1-pound) red snapper fillet (completely boneless)
1 (14- to 16-ounce) can tomatoes (Cento brand preferred)
Salt and freshly ground black pepper
5 to 6 fresh basil leaves, torn

Coat the bottom of a frying pan with olive oil. Add butter and melt over moderate heat. Sauté the snapper fillet skin side up for one minute. (No longer, just long enough to seal the juices.) Remove the fish from the pan and set on a warm platter. Put the tomatoes in the pan and let cook, stirring occasionally, for five minutes, adding salt and pepper to taste. Put the fish back in the sauce, skin side down, and baste while cooking. Add the basil leaves and continue to cook until fish is done.

Serves 2 to 4.

$\mathcal{C}$HARLOTTE, NORTH CAROLINA, was a clean-looking city, but I was kind of lonesome, having no friends at that time in my life, and having to meet new ones. It was difficult for me because I was a stranger and almost everyone is skeptical to talk to a stranger, much less trust him. So it was always the bar or club scene, offering cocktails to the ladies, telling one-liner jokes, etc. I met this attractive young lady in a club called Happens. She was alone sitting at the bar. I had been going to Happens for a month now, and this is the first time I saw her. She seemed to have a whipped look on her face. I offered her a drink and she accepted. We started to talk and to my surprise she didn't ask me the usual bull crap questions that I generally hear. In fact, I was the aggressive one and started to ask her the same questions that I usually have to answer. Her name was Lori de Jesus, and her parents came from Brazil. An aunt had raised her, and sent her off to school in Connecticut until she became of age. After she graduated, Lori went to nursing school because she wanted to become a nurse. At the age of twenty-three she gave up nursing and, to cut the story short, worked as a waitress until she met this— what she thought was a wonderful man, and married him. She told me that he wasn't that wonderful after all. He was lazy, drunk most of the time, and he beat her a lot. To look at her you wouldn't believe that this beautiful creature was beaten that badly. Her skin was as smooth as silk, and her long, straight blond hair was below her shoulders. Lori never had any children and that explained her knockout figure. She stood five-feet, seven inches in height and she said her weight was between 117 and 120 pounds. I liked her. She was nice company. She told me she was thirty years old, and she was divorced. I told her I was a half-assed chef and that I'd like to cook a snack for her sometime. Lori agreed and off we went to an all-night supermarket, bought the groceries, and then drove to my apartment. Lori loved the taste of clams.

Clams Oregano

2 (10-ounce) cans whole baby clams or 24 fresh littleneck
   clams
½ cup finely chopped onion
4 to 6 cloves garlic minced
Extra-virgin olive oil
½ cup plain bread crumbs
½ cup finely chopped fresh parsley
1 tablespoon dried oregano

Empty clamshells (if using canned clams)
Freshly grated Romano or Parmesan cheese (optional)
Paprika (optional)
Lemon wedges

If you're using canned clams, drain them and reserve the juice. If you have fresh clams, open them over a strainer placed in a bowl. Save the clams, juices, and shells.

Sauté the onions and garlic in a little olive oil until translucent. In a large bowl put the clam juice, bread crumbs, sautéed garlic and onions, chopped parsley, and oregano. Mix thoroughly. The mixture should be moist and hold together, almost like a paste. Place the clams in the half-shells, and cover completely with the bread crumb mixture. Bake at 350 to 375 degrees for 20 minutes. Just before serving, sprinkle cheese or paprika over the tops and broil until slightly brown. Serve immediately with a wedge of lemon on the side.

Makes 24 pieces.

I MET A COUPLE of guys my age and we played golf together about three or four times a week. It was chance for me to spend some time with my Yorkshire terrier, Giuseppe. He looked forward to riding in the cart with me. I was teaching him to grab the ball in his mouth and put it behind a tree or hide it somewhere. He learned how to carry the ball in his mouth all right, but the animal only grabbed mine and used to drop it in the water. Go figure. I ended that project quickly.

I had noticed that the local police were always eyeing me. I naturally wondered why. I mean, I never went over the speed limit. I was a very careful driver. Whenever I went out on a date I would always ask my date if she was a heavy drinker and if so I'd hire a driver to chauffeur us, otherwise she would drive. This one early evening I was stopped by a police officer. Giuseppe, my pet, had his normal position on my lap. So when the cop signaled me to the curb, I was surprised.

"Let me see your driver's license and automobile registration, please." The cop was an African American, built big and strong, like a brick ____ house.

"What's wrong, officer?" I demanded to know. "Why did you stop me?"

"Well, sir, I was just wondering, are you able to handle your car properly with that there animal on your lap like that? Especially in all this here traffic," he asked very politely.

I thought for a minute, "All these old farts, especially the women, who drive with their pets on their lap, probably never getting stopped," I said to him, having a little fun of course. "Officer, I'd like to ask you a few questions concerning the vehicle that my Yorkie and I are in, if that's all right with you."

"Of course, sir, and I'll be glad to answer them if I can."

"Was the car speeding, or was the driving erratic or maybe the car crossed over the yellow line?"

"Oh no, sir. It ain't anything like that. I was just wondering if y'all was handling the car all right."

"Oh, thank god that's all it is because you see, officer, this Yorkie is my designated driver and if you said he wasn't driving that well, I'd have to fire him. As it is, he's on probation."

Well, you had to see that cop's face. He looked embarrassed and said "Y'all drive careful now." He left with a smile on his face.

"Nice guy," I said to myself. I went to my apartment and fixed myself something to eat.

Linguine with White Clam Sauce

½ pound linguine
6 tablespoons extra-virgin olive oil
2 tablespoons butter
2 cloves garlic, minced
1 shallot, minced
1 teaspoon flour
½ cup dry white wine
12 fresh littleneck clams, freshly opened (reserve juice), or
    1 (10-ounce) can baby clams
Juice of ½ lemon
Salt and freshly ground black pepper to taste
1 (8-ounce) bottle Doxsee clam juice (optional; see Note)

Cook the linguine al dente. When done, drain and sprinkle 2 tablespoons olive oil over it and twirl to coat the pasta to prevent sticking together. Set aside.

In a large frying pan, melt half the butter with 4 tablespoons of the olive oil. Sauté the garlic and shallot lightly. Place the flour with the remaining butter in a small pan and stir over low heat to make a roux. Add the roux to the large frying pan and stir. Add the wine and clams with their juice and stir. Squeeze the lemon over the clams. Cook for a few minutes, stirring, until mixture forms a smooth blend. Add salt and pepper to taste, then add the pasta to the pan and stir around until all linguine is saturated with sauce. Serve immediately.

Serves 1 to 2.

NOTE: If there isn't enough clam juice from the clams to make a smooth sauce, use a portion of the bottled clam juice.

$\mathcal{N}$OVEMBER, 1993: it's exactly four months to the day that I leased the apartment. I had two more months on my lease. Alice the apartment manager was after me to renew my rental contract.

"I'm looking to buy something in this lovely city, Alice. So I'll let you know next month," I said to her. Of course that was an untruth, as I never knew in advance whether or not I had to pack up and leave.

The heat was still on me, and I couldn't get any help from anyone. I started to watch how I was spending my money, because I had no money coming in at all. I was still seeing Lori occasionally. She started to become a little too possessive. Asking me where I was going, what time will I be home, was I seeing other women? *"Madrone,* she was getting to be like a wife. Fuhgedaboudit," I said to the wall I was looking at.

I couldn't tell her about my life. I couldn't and wouldn't trust anyone. How could I? Don't misunderstand me. Lori was someone you would want to take home to mother, so to speak. She wasn't only beautiful, she was smart, clean, and the most charming person I met in my lifestyle. But Lori wanted commitment. How could I possibly give her that? I expected to be whacked sometime or other and to this day I still do. I didn't want to involve her. The mob doesn't forgive or forget. I had one thing going for me in that aspect: I don't either. So that's why I was thinking of leaving the area. I had to get Lori out of my system and I no longer would be living at heaven's manor or anywhere in North Carolina. I started to go to the library to look for information on different states. I zeroed in on Birmingham, Alabama, because it had a racetrack. I called Lori up and invited her over for dessert and coffee. "Yes, honey, real dessert. Something that I'm preparing," I said.

Strawberries with Grand Marnier Sauce

1 pound ripe strawberries, hulled
2 ounces Grand Marnier
1 tablespoon sugar
Juice of ½ lemon
2 to 3 ounces balsamic vinegar

Slice the berries and place them with all the other ingredients in a bowl. Toss or mix easily, so as not to crush the berries. Cover and marinate at room temperature for two hours. Transfer to a pot and heat over moderate flame for 3 to 4 minutes, tossing gently. Serve over ice cream.

Serves 6.

My YORKIE, Giuseppe, and I drove to Birmingham, Alabama; I wanted to see what it was like. We checked in at a Ramada Inn. I inquired how to get to the dog track and I went there to make a few wagers. I lost, naturally. I met a few people and while talking, I found out that Hoover was a decent place to live. After the races, I went back to the Ramada Inn and took Giuseppe for a walk. I gave the security guard a few bucks to keep an eye out for my pet while I was gone. I had to sneak the dog into the room because no pets were allowed. It was safe—that no one would notice, as the manager left the area at four in the afternoon daily. I obtained this information from the clerk when I tipped her ten bucks to let Giuseppe in. When I awoke, I showered and got on the road to look at some rentals. I was having a hard time getting around, so I went to a real estate office and they helped me locate an apartment. The rents were cheaper than Charlotte, which I was glad about, but the rental places were not as nice either. Birmingham, to me, looked like a very poor city. The state had a sales tax of over 8 percent on everything, even on your groceries. I felt sorry for the poor African Americans. Probably the politicians didn't give a damn about the people. They gave you nothing for that tax money either. Look at a southern state like Florida. It's beautiful, clean, and their sales taxes are less than Alabama's or Georgia's, and Florida doesn't charge taxes on groceries. "There's something wrong here," I said to myself. New York City has a little bit higher sales tax, but look at the difference. In New York if it snows your streets are plowed, sanded, and made to drive on. They had a little snow drop in Birmingham one winter while I was there and they closed the main highway down. Go figure! Anyway I had to make the best of my life, so I rented a two-bedroom apartment for $475 a month. It was all right. It was not as nice as the other place I still had in North Carolina, but hey!

I gave the rental manager a month's rent, plus a $250 cleaning deposit, and told him I would be moving in in five weeks, on January 2, 1994. All was agreeable. He gave me a set of keys and I started on my four-hour trip back to Charlotte. I noticed a pretty neighbor living there, while I was looking at the apartments.

"It probably won't be that bad living there," I thought to myself. I had to figure what to tell Lori and my golf buddies—it would be all lies of course. But hey! What else can I do? When I arrived home in Charlotte, I went to the store to pick up a few groceries, to make myself a snack. I felt like having a salad, so I thought I'd make my own dressing, and have some left over in the event Lori wanted to try it. It's the best vinaigrette I have ever had. I got the recipe from the chef who worked in a sandwich shop out west somewhere. I watched how he made it and then he showed me the recipe.

Herbed Vinaigrette

3 tablespoons soy sauce (preferably tamari)
1 cup apple cider vinegar
2 tablespoons dehydrated minced onions
½ cup chopped fresh parsley
2 cups extra-virgin olive oil
2 tablespoons minced garlic
3 tablespoons tahini (sesame butter)
3 shakes dulse-kelp-nori (seaweed seasoning)

Put all the ingredients in a screw-top jar and shake vigorously. Serve at room temperature over salad. Keep in refrigerator.

Makes about 3½ cups.

NOTE: Tahini, tamari, and seaweed seasoning can be found in health food stores.

I DIDN'T SAY anything to Lori about my moving. I didn't know what or how to tell her. "Should I be honest with her," I pondered in my thoughts, "or come up with some lamebrain excuse?" I had to tell her something. She was too good for me. I only had seven or eight days left. I was almost all packed, everything except my dishes, pots and pans, utensils, and clothes were in the spare bedroom. Lori had asked once,

"Why do you always keep that door locked? Are you hiding something or someone from me?"

"You clocked it, Lori! You're so intelligent. I have a broad in there that takes care of me some more, after you're through with me. Didn't you know that I was King Kong? I need two, not one, broad a day to satisfy me completely." She went to the door and started kicking it and yelling obscenities, because she believed me. I laughed like hell, but the only way I could relieve her was to unlock the door and let her see for herself. She started to punch the hell out of my body, because I couldn't control my laughter.

I came to a decision. I was going to tell her who I was, and if she accepted it I would send for her, and get married. I called her and asked her if she would have dinner with me the next night. She accepted but only if I fixed something light, like a salad. I agreed. It was a day before Christmas Eve, December 23. So I had an appropriate snack.

Christmas Salad

DRESSING
2½ cups extra-virgin olive oil
½ cup sugar
1 cup red wine vinegar
1 teaspoon prepared mustard
½ teaspoon garlic salt
1 teaspoon poppy seeds

SALAD

1 large head romaine lettuce, washed, dried, and torn into
    bite-size pieces
6 ounces fancy Swiss cheese, shredded
1 cup cashews
About 20 seedless grapes, cut in half
1 pound bacon, cooked crisp, drained, and crumbled

Put all the dressing ingredients in a screw-top jar and shake
well. Marinate in the refrigerator for 3 to 5 hours before
using. Combine all the salad ingredients in a large bowl.
Pour the dressing over the salad, toss repeatedly, and serve.

Serves 4 to 6.

$\mathcal{L}$ORI CAME OVER with Christmas gifts, so after dinner we
exchanged presents. She was always well dressed, and she
looked great even in jeans. She asked me for the Christmas
salad recipe. Whenever I introduced that dressing to anyone,
they always wanted to know how to make it. So if it was on
my bill of fare I'd type out the ingredients and details and
have it ready for them when they asked.

Lori's gifts were nice. She got me an expensive wallet,
Polo cologne, and a gold set of cufflinks. The links were

beautiful. "You should not have spent all that money on me, honey. These cufflinks are too expensive, and so is the billfold. I love all the gifts, but I feel a little uncomfortable accepting them."

"What about the gifts you bought for me? The diamond earrings are the best gift that I ever received. And all of the other stuff, also. I think you overdid it." We talked about small stuff, admiring each other, and then I brought her to the spare bedroom where everything was packed, and told her I was leaving the area.

"But Joe, why are you leaving? I was looking forward to a future with you."

I sat her down and explained everything to her. How the mob tried to kill me, about my undercover work, everything. I told Lori that if she wanted to come with me she'd be more than welcome and I expressed my feelings for her. "I care for you an awful lot. I know that if your decision is negative, I will be hurt by your choice. But in all fairness to you, it would be the right decision." I told maybe too much but I couldn't be selfish. She looked rejected and whipped. She told me she would have to think this all out and she would let me know what she decided. I told her that I would not try and influence her in any way, and that I would wait to hear from her. And left it like that. Lori and I kissed good night and her face was wet with tears.

Lori never called. As I was about to leave, the same time the moving van was, I telephoned Lori to say goodbye. A recording came on stating that the phone number was disconnected. "Just as well," I thought. "I'll just move on."

—⸰⸰—

BIRMINGHAM was a friendly place. The people seemed to be very nice and helpful. There was a large African-American population living in that city. And the majority of the African Americans were almost poverty stricken, from what I could see. There were quite a few good old boys in that city, also. In the first six months I was there, I didn't do too much except go to the Birmingham racetrack once in a while. I cooked for the pretty neighbors a couple of times. The first dish I made for them was for a party of about ten people, and we were all supposed to bring something. I knew very little about country cooking so one of the neighbors whose name was Julie Brown helped me with this dish. In fact she did most of it.

King Ranch Chicken

3 pounds boneless and skinless chicken
3 to 4 cups chicken broth
1 medium onion, chopped
1 (10.75-ounce) can cream of chicken soup
1 (10.75-ounce) can cream of mushroom soup
2 (10-ounce) cans Rotel tomatoes (or other diced tomatoes
*   with chilies)*
1 (4-ounce) can chopped green chilies
2 tablespoons chili powder

1 tablespoon garlic powder
Salt and pepper
Vegetable oil cooking spray
Tortilla chips
Shredded Monterey Jack cheese
Shredded Cheddar cheese

Place the chicken in a large saucepan and add chicken broth to cover. Boil the chicken until it's cooked through. Remove from the liquid and cool. Save the broth. When the chicken has cooled slightly, shred it and set aside. In the broth, place the onion. Cook over moderate flame until onion is tender. Add the soups along with the tomatoes, green chilies, and chili and garlic powders. Add salt and pepper to taste. Simmer for about 15 minutes, stirring occasionally.

Spray a 9 by 13-inch baking dish thoroughly with vegetable oil cooking spray. Cover the bottom of the dish with sauce. Add a layer of the chips on top of the sauce, then the cheeses, some chicken, and finally sauce again. Repeat this process until the chicken is finished. Pour any remaining sauce over the top. Bake at 350 degrees for 45 minutes.

Serves 8 to 10.

HERE'S ANOTHER DISH that I made for Mia, another one of my neighbors.

Brook Trout Amandine

1 tablespoon melted butter
2 tablespoons extra-virgin olive oil
1 freshwater trout, gutted and cleaned
Salt and pepper
4 to 5 lettuce leaves (wilted ones are okay)
½ cup sliced almonds

In a metal oven platter, place the melted butter along with the olive oil. Wash and dry the fish in cold water only, cavity included. Salt and pepper the trout on both sides. Place the fish on the platter, turning it so that the oil and butter are all over the fish. The trout should be lying on its side with cavity opening facing the left or right. Place the lettuce over the trout, making sure the body of the fish is covered from head to tail (you thought I was going to say *toe*, didn't you?). Put the platter under the broiler about 6 to 8 inches below the flame, for 7 to 8 minutes. Check occasionally by lifting a lettuce leaf and puncturing the fish with a toothpick. When the fish is done, remove the leaves and discard them. Sprinkle the almonds over the fish evenly, baste with the juices, and put under the broiler for 45 seconds to 1 minute, until almonds are toasted. Garnish the dish with dark grapes or any small piece of fruit. Serve while hot.

Serves 1.

Apple and Blueberry Cobbler

4 cups peeled, sliced Granny Smith apples (3 to 4 apples)
1 pint fresh blueberries, rinsed and drained
½ cup melted butter
2¼ cups sugar
1 tablespoon cornstarch
1 cup flour
2 tablespoons baking powder
1 cup heavy cream
2 to 3 tablespoons cinnamon (to your taste)

Cook the apples and blueberries with 2 tablespoons of the butter, 1 cup of the sugar, and the cornstarch dissolved in 2 cups of water, stirring frequently for 5 to 6 minutes over moderate heat. Sift together the flour and baking powder. Add 1 cup of the sugar and the cream and stir until it forms into a smooth batter. Put the rest of the melted butter into a 10 by 6-inch ovenproof glass dish; spread evenly on the bottom. Pour the batter on top of the butter. Spread the apples, blueberries, and liquid over the batter carefully and evenly. Mix the cinnamon and remaining ¼ cup sugar together and sprinkle over the fruit. Bake at 350 degrees for 30 to 35 minutes.

Serves 6 to 8.

I WAS IN BIRMINGHAM for three months now, and it was very boring for me. It was a city where it was hard to get close to anyone, much less be their friend. I was in a shell. If I didn't have my Yorkie, Giuseppe, I would have jumped out my window headfirst. But then again I would have only dirtied my clothes, because I lived on the ground floor. I was short of cash, and I noticed a jewelry store in the neighborhood where I lived. So I moseyed my way over there, and met the owner. I started to ingratiate myself to him, and he gave me some money for some hot jewelry that I had. Of course, he didn't know that it was hot. To me at the time he was a godsend. About a year later, I gave him one of my cookbooks and autographed it to his wife. A couple of weeks later, I happened to be in his store and he asked me if any of the stories were true. I took a chance and told him. "They're all true," I said, glaring in his eyes.

You have got to remember, I'd been living a life of deception and been very secretive about everything that I've done since the beginning of 1981. I was in a state of depression for periods at a time. I missed male friendship. I missed talking to people. Oh, sure, I had dates with quite a few young ladies, but that was different. I cooked for them and had some fun. But I missed shooting the breeze with the guys and having a few drinks with them, and so on.

That's why I took the chance on telling the jeweler about myself. I gave him a copy of the A&E tape of me and he asked me if I would speak at the club he belonged to. He said he would order a bunch of my biography books and cookbooks also, and whatever profits he made he would split it with me. So I went and he played the tape. At first, people were squirming in their seats. But everyone was fascinated, and had a good time. The jeweler sold about fifty books, and I never saw a dime. So I went to his store a week later and said to him, "Did you read my autobiography? And if you did, do you think I'm going to let you take advantage of me on the sales of those books? Where is my share of the money?" I said this to him in a low but stern voice. He stuttered and fumbled and then handed me $200, telling me that he forgot. "Go figure," I said to myself.

I was walking my good pal, Giuseppe, in the shopping center across the street from where I resided, when the jeweler came running out of his store. "Joe, there's a woman in my place who wants you to autograph your book. She wants to buy the last one I have, and she'd like to have it signed by you. I told her I didn't know if you had left town or not, and then I spotted you walking." I followed him to his store and saw this attractive young lady standing there.

"What is your name, miss, and please spell it for me," I asked.

"Oh, it's not for me, It's for my husband. He's an avid reader on the Mafia. He knows all about you mob guys" she said, smiling. "His name is Tommy."

I signed the book for her and said "Thank you, Carolyn," the name she introduced herself as. She also said she would purchase the cookbook at Books-A-Million.

Approximately a week later I got a call from the jeweler. "Joe, do you remember the lady that you signed that cookbook for at my store? Her name is Carolyn?" I told him I did. "Well, her husband would like to have you call him, at his restaurant. I think he wants to meet up with you." The jeweler gave me the number to call. I just put it aside and pondered over the idea of contacting him. I would have loved to meet a few guys and shoot the breeze with them, so to speak, but I was very paranoid. There was a high-priced contract out on my head and I didn't want to make anyone rich. Not off my life, anyway. So I let it slide, for the moment.

"JOEY, what time do you want us to come to dinner?" Margarita asked me. She was a very pretty Spanish lady who I had become friends with. Margarita lived in the same complex as I. She was coming to dinner with a couple of her girlfriends and we were going to eat first and then party together. I supplied all the food and some of the wine, and they brought the hard booze and their other goodies, in which I didn't participate. Well, some of it I didn't.

"Be here at 7:00 P.M. for cocktails and hors d'oeuvres." I was going to make stuffed mushrooms.

Mushrooms Stuffed with Crabmeat

1 cup flour
20 small mushrooms
1 (8-ounce) can lump white crabmeat
1 teaspoon garlic powder
1 shallot, chopped fine
4 tablespoons extra-virgin olive oil
½ cup chopped fresh Italian parsley
1 sleeve Ritz crackers, crushed into crumbs
Juice of ½ lemon
8 tablespoons (1 stick) butter, melted
Salt and freshly ground black pepper
½ cup dry white wine

In a sink, place approximately 2 gallons cold water; put the flour in the water and then the mushrooms. Swish the mushrooms around for a minute or two. Remove the stems from the mushrooms. Keep 10 stems and discard the others. Rinse off the mushrooms and pat dry with a paper towel. Chop the reserved stems very fine.

Open the can of crabmeat and place in a 3-quart bowl, separating it with a fork. Put the garlic powder on top of the crabmeat. Sauté the shallot and the mushroom stems in the olive oil for 3 minutes over medium heat and then add to the crab. Add the parsley and the Ritz crumbs and toss thoroughly. Add the lemon juice, melted butter, and salt and pepper to taste and mix well. It should be a pasty mixture.

Fill the caps with the crab mixture. Arrange in a shallow baking dish with the white wine on the bottom of the pan. Bake at 350 degrees for 20 to 25 minutes.

Makes 20 pieces.

AFTER EATING the stuffed mushrooms, I went in the kitchen for the next dish that I was going to cook. A young lady named Julie Hawkins had given me the recipe and the instructions on how to prepare and cook this delightful dish. She works for the United States government. (I thought she might be a C.I.A. agent.) I met her on a Southwest airplane. She was traveling from Alabama to Texas, on her way back to the San Antonio army base. She is now based in Japan and she keeps in touch with me; we e-mail each other once in awhile.

I remember the time I met her in the Birmingham airport. I made a move on her and she laughed at me, saying "You're old enough to be my dad." She's a fantastic lady. It was the most pleasant flight I ever had. Julie looks at me like I'm her Uncle Joe. I looked at her wishing I were born twelve to fifteen years later. I was crazy about this young, pretty, charming *bambina*, "But, hey, I can dream, can't I," I said, pondering.

Julie's Pasta Primavera with Shrimp

1 pound linguine pasta
1 cup broccoli florets
¼ cup extra-virgin olive oil
1 pound medium shrimp, peeled and deveined
1 each red, yellow, and orange bell pepper, cut into quarters and sliced thin
1 cup green beans cut into 1-inch pieces
5 asparagus spears, cut into 1-inch pieces
1 cup sugar snap peas
3 cloves garlic, minced
Salt and freshly ground black pepper
1 pint grape tomatoes, cut in half
2 cups fresh basil cut into strips
½ cup freshly grated Romano cheese
2 tablespoons freshly grated lemon peel

Boil lightly salted water and cook the pasta al dente, following the instructions on the package. One minute before the pasta is done, add the broccoli. Reserve ¾ cup of the water, then drain the remaining water from the pasta. Set aside. Meanwhile heat I tablespoon of the olive oil in a large skillet over medium heat. Add the shrimp and cook 2 to 3 minutes, tossing from side to side. Remove the shrimp and set aside.

Heat the remaining oil in the same skillet. Add the peppers, beans, asparagus, peas, garlic, and salt and pepper to taste. Sauté 4 to 5 minutes until the vegetables are tender-crisp. Stir in the reserved cooking water, the grape tomatoes, and the shrimp, and cook I to 2 minutes, until heated through.

Return the pasta and broccoli to the pot they were cooked in, add the mixture from the skillet and the basil, cheese, and lemon peel, and toss until all the pasta is coated with sauce. Serve immediately.

Serves 4.

Kessene's Caramelized Peaches Italian–Style

4 large ripe fresh peaches
½ cup Amaretto Disaronno
12 tablespoons (1½ sticks) unsalted butter
¾ cup raw sugar or light brown sugar
8 amaretti cookies, crushed

Cut the peaches in half and remove the pits. Place in an ovenproof baking dish cut side up. Pour the amaretto over the peaches and marinate.

In a small saucepan over medium heat, melt the butter and add the sugar. Heat until the mixture becomes bubbly and the sugar melts and begins to caramelize. Be careful not to burn! Remove from the heat and carefully pour the caramel mixture over the peaches. Sprinkle the crushed cookies over the peaches. Cover with aluminum foil and bake in a preheated 350-degree oven for 30 minutes. Serve warm and top with fresh whipped cream.

Serves 8.

$\sim$ ᏟᎿᎾ $\sim$

$\mathcal{M}$Y JEWELER FRIEND called me about a week later and said "Joe, that guy's wife, you know the one who wanted to meet you, called and asked if I would please tell you to call her husband. He wants to meet you and buy you a drink. She said that he never met a wiseguy before. All he ever does is read about you guys." He gave me the phone number again and I thought about it for a couple of days and then decided to give him a call. The jeweler told me his name was Tommy Ray.

"Hello, is Tommy Ray there?"

"Who's calling?" the pleasant voice that answered asked.

"Tell him it's Joe Dogs," I answered.

A pause, then "Hello, is that you Joe?" the voice asked.

I didn't say anything for approximately five to eight seconds because I was apprehensive. I was worried that maybe I didn't do the right thing by exposing my identity to a total stranger. Those five to eight seconds seemed like an hour to me.

"Hello, hello! Joe! Are you there?" the voice continued. Not a harsh or nasty voice, but a friendly one.

"Yes. Hi, Tommy, the jeweler told me that you wanted to meet me, and I have to be perfectly honest with you, Tom, I'm skeptical on whom I indulge in any conversations with. I'm sure you can understand why." I said.

"Of course I do, Joe. You can trust me with your life. You're one of my heroes. When my wife purchased your book, I told her I already read it. I went out and bought it right away as soon as it hit the streets. I'm an avid reader of you Mafia guys. I hate them, though, and I would be proud to meet you. You did a number on those SOBs. Look, Joe, I own this place called The Hearth. You're welcome here anytime as my guest. We have great food and drinks. You think it over and you come here whenever you feel comfortable."

We talked for about ten more minutes and all the while I was trying to get a read on him but it was impossible. I said goodbye and told him I would be in touch. Tommy Ray gave me his home phone number and his other business number. He owned and operated a printing press business that employed between fifty and sixty people. It was called Ray Press. Although I only talked to him on the phone, I liked him. He seemed like a warm person and I was hungry for friendship. I was in a shell, and I wanted out of it. I didn't want to endanger myself, though. The jeweler was the only one who knew who I was and he opened his mouth to how many, I don't know. Now Tommy Ray knew. I hoped that he wouldn't reveal who I was to the patrons at his bar, but that was impossible. Again I pondered over the situation that I put myself in.

Two weeks went by and I was calling Tommy Ray about every other day, promising him I would be coming there to meet him. I had gotten friendly with his female bartender, Donna, so we talked a little whenever I called. I was apprehensive, but I wanted to go. The only place I went to was the dog track, and I was sick of that.

It was August, 1995. I had been in Birmingham, Alabama, for eighteen months. I had landed a job as a security officer—

it was relatively easy to get. I lied like a trooper on the application. They never checked it out so I was in. The job paid next to nothing, but I had to eat, and the work was actually very easy. There was nothing to do but sit wherever you were posted and look stupid. Maybe walk the post once in awhile. I didn't mention to Tommy that I was working as a security guard. I worked nights, so it was impossible to go to his place of business.

"*I*'LL HAVE A Dewar's Scotch on the rocks, please" I said to the pretty bartender, who I had learned was Donna. The place was crowded. It was a rather small bar with tables crowded into the room and a large round table with about ten to twelve people around it drinking, laughing, and being loud. They seemed to be having a good time. I wore a black leather jacket trying to fit the place and the atmosphere. I looked around, went to the bathroom, and looked in the dining room which was crowded with patrons eating. I returned to the bar and struck up a conversation with Donna. She knew immediately that I was from up North, from my voice. I had to be careful. "Here I am in the Deep South, not knowing anyone. God only knows if they're still fighting the Civil War over here," I thought to myself. "Donna, is the owner, Tommy Ray, in tonight?" I asked her.

"Yeah, he's right there. That's the guy, with the long hair, sitting with his back towards us at the big table. I think I know who you are now," Donna said, smiling.

I smiled back and walked over to the table and put a paperback Joe Dogs book in front of Tommy Ray. I had retrieved it from inside my leather jacket. Tommy looked up, I smiled, and we shook hands. He introduced me to everyone in the place, and all of a sudden I was not in that shell any longer. I felt as if an albatross had been lifted from my shoulders. I was feeling great. Tommy made me feel relaxed. He said, "Don't worry about those mob guys. We all carry guns in this bar."

I stayed with Tommy talking and drinking until the wee hours—it was the first time in fifteen years that I felt comfortable. I went home and slept like a baby. I didn't have to report for work until 8 P.M., so I could sleep all day. I took Giuseppe for a walk and fed him, and off to sleep I went. I was famished when I woke up so I cooked for Giuseppe and for myself.

Meat Loaf with Pork

1 shallot, chopped fine
¼ cup finely chopped celery
¼ cup finely chopped carrot
Extra-virgin olive oil
½ pound ground beef
½ pound ground pork

½ cup tomato sauce *(Hunt's preferred)* or ¼ cup ketchup
  (Heinz preferred)
1 jumbo egg
Salt and freshly ground black pepper
Bread crumbs as needed

Sauté the shallots, celery, and carrot in extra-virgin olive oil in a frying pan over moderate heat until translucent. Set aside. In a large bowl, mix together the beef and pork, sautéed vegetables, tomato sauce, and egg, mixing thoroughly. Add salt and pepper to taste. If mixture feels too wet, add bread crumbs and mix until you get the right texture. Shape into an oval and put in a shallow baking pan with a ½ cup water in the bottom of the pan. Bake in a preheated oven at 350 degrees for 50 minutes, or until done. Remove from the oven and let stand for 10 minutes before serving. This recipe goes well with brown gravy.

Serves 4.

BROWN GRAVY

2 tablespoons drippings from the meat loaf pan
2 tablespoons flour
½ to 1 cup beef or vegetable stock
½ cup milk or cream
Salt and freshly ground black pepper

In a small frying pan or pot mix the drippings and flour together to make a roux. Cook, stirring, until slightly brown. Add the milk or cream, stirring constantly. Add enough stock to form the right texture. Add salt and pepper to taste and cook 5 minutes longer, stirring. Serve over meat loaf immediately.

I HAD BEEN GOING to the Hearth for about a month. I was working four days a week, twelve hours a day. So I could go to Tommy's place three nights a week. I was ashamed to tell him I was a night watchman. I came to find out later that if Tommy liked you, he didn't care what you did for a living as long as you were straight with him.

Tommy Ray had a Christmas party and invited about 150 people to the shindig. I was invited also, but I was too paranoid to show up. Tommy was disappointed as he told a lot of people I would be there. He called me his Pet Mobster. We got along swell.

It was in February, 1996, I was on my way to my security job. It was raining very hard. The skies really opened up. I was almost at my destination, when a car pulls out in front of me. He must have driven through his stop sign. He forced me to brake hard, but not quick enough because I smashed him broadside. My head hit the windshield, and the driver of the other car took off. Luckily there was a patrolman who saw the accident. I had no insurance and neither did the other driver. In Alabama it was not mandatory to have insurance at that time. They've changed the insurance laws since then.

My mind was thinking a million miles an hour. I had a problem now. I had no money put aside. I had a different identification for the veterans' hospital than my driver's license. An ambulance arrived and the police officer gave him the name that was on the driver's license. He radioed in and they responded negatively to that name. The ambulance driver stopped the vehicle and said that I couldn't go there " 'cause they don't know you." I told him I forgot to tell the cop of my name change and gave him the proper name that showed up on the computer. The government had me so screwed up I didn't know what name to give anyone. When I got on the stretcher my .38 pistol fell out of my pocket and a security guard confiscated it, asking me if I had a permit or license to carry. I lied to them and told them I left it home. "Well, you just come here with your license whenever you want to pick it up," the guard said.

My head hurt and I didn't know what I was going to do. Everything was going through my mind. How was I going to get to work, no wheels, no gun, and no money? I was in trouble. I didn't know where I was. How was I going to get home? I called the Hearth Restaurant from the stretcher I was lying on. The orderly handed me the phone.

"Hello, is Tommy there?" I asked the person answering the phone.

"Just a moment," she replied.

"Hello?"

"Hello, Tom, listen—I was in an automobile accident. My

car is demolished. Could you please come to the VA hospital and pick me up and give me a lift home? I hate to bother you but you're the only person I know in Birmingham that I could call."

"All right, Joe Dogs, stop fooling around. Come on over for a drink."

"Honest to God, Tom, here, the doctor will tell you," I said, handing him the phone. The doctor confirmed my statement and he handed me back the phone. Tommy apologized and was at the hospital in less than fifteen minutes. While he was waiting for me he went to the security office and retrieved my .38 with his pistol license. Once in the car Tommy handed me back my gun, and said to me "Let's go to the Hearth and have a drink."

"Gee Tom, I don't know. I have no wheels. I have no money. I don't know what to do. I don't have anyone here that I can ask for help. I had to take this security job to put food on the table, and now I have to give it up, because how in God's name am I going to get to my job? It's very embarrassing that I'm bothering you with all this here. I'd love to have a drink. I could use one. Will you give me a lift home when you close?"

"Yeah, don't worry. You can take this car home with you tonight. Give me a lift home after we close and then drive yourself home. You can meet me tomorrow and I'll see what I can do for you with some sort of transportation."

"This guy was a godsend. Especially now," I was thinking out loud.

Tommy and I locked up his place of business and I drove him home. He lived on the top of a hill or mountain and had a view of the city of Birmingham and more. The view was breathtaking. Tommy and I had had a few drinks, so I drove carefully. "He's quite a guy, and very generous," I said to myself.

I met Tommy the next day for lunch with some of his employees, and he told me that he didn't have any luck with an automobile for me. So he said "You just go ahead and keep driving the Taurus. Only be careful with the gears. You New Yorkers don't know how to drive a stick shift." Everyone laughed at Tom's remark and he made me feel as if I belonged. Tommy told me to chuck the security job, and to ask Donna if she could use me in the kitchen for lunch and dinner. "Donna's the boss. I don't want to step on her toes. If she says okay then I'll give you ten bucks an hour to start. Is that all right with you? You won't have to do any clean-up, let the other people do that. You make the special for the day. Whaddya say?"

"Yeah! Of course. When do you want me to start? I could start tomorrow if you want," I said. That was twice as much as I was making as a guard.

"I told you: first you have to get the okay from Donna. Ask her when she wants you to start. I'll even order a bunch of your books, and we can sell them here. You can keep the profit and I'll just take back my investment. The people who come in here will probably buy over a hundred of them. Order me two dozen of each."

I gave Tom all the information on how to order the books, and he relayed it all to his executive secretary, whom he addressed as "E Woman." I found out later that her name was Elaine. She more or less ran the business for Tommy Ray. I liked her. She was a straight-from-the-shoulder person. Elaine told it like it was, with no remorse.

I talked with Donna that evening and it was no problem. Donna was a very pretty young lady, a divorcée with an extremely beautiful eighteen-year-old daughter. To look at her, I felt she ought to be in movies. She was a polite young lady, and also had a daughter. I very seldom saw her.

I started working the following week. I met the kitchen crew. They were mostly African Americans. There were Pops and his wife Doris Anne, and two of their sons. They were all very receptive to me and there were no problems, although Pops did not get along well with the general manager, whose name was Ali something or other. He was from Iraq and I didn't like him either, so I stayed away from him as much as I could. Tommy advised Pops, who was in charge of the kitchen, that I was to cook the daily lunch special and none of the other stuff. I in turn advised Pops that if we get busy, I would gladly pitch in and help wherever I was needed. That statement to Pops put a smile on his face. Tommy advised me to cook something affordable as he got an extremely large crowd of office workers for lunch. So I talked it over with Pops and we decided on a chicken gumbo. I had gotten this recipe from F.B.I. Agent Charlie Beaudoin who was stationed with an organized crime unit in the Manhattan office, New York. He gave it to me while we were on a stakeout pertaining to the Gambino organized crime family. This is for four to six people. Of course, I made a much larger batch.

Chicken Gumbo

1 pound spicy Italian or kielbasa sausage
1 pound boneless and skinless chicken
6 cups chicken stock
1 cup chopped onion
1 cup chopped green bell pepper
1 cup chopped celery
1 cup peeled, sliced broccoli stalks
2 cloves garlic, chopped
1/4 teaspoon cayenne pepper
1 teaspoon freshly ground black pepper
1/2 teaspoon dried tyme
1 1/2 teaspoons salt
1/4 teaspoon dried oregano
2 bay leaves
2 tablespoons brown gravy or roux mix
1 tablespoon Wondra flour
1 tablespoon softened butter
1 teaspoon ground sassafras leaf

In a soup pot, cover the chicken and sausage with the chicken stock and simmer until almost done. Reserve 5 to 6 cups of the stock and discard the balance. Allow the meat to cool, then slice the sausage and cut the chicken into bite-size pieces. Return the reserved stock to the pot. Add the spicy sausage slices and chicken pieces and bring the stock to a boil. Add the onion, bell pepper, celery, broccoli, garlic, cayenne, black pepper, thyme, salt, oregano, bay leaves and brown gravy mix. Cook until the vegetables are cooked but firm. Place the flour in a bowl with the butter and mix together forming a paste. Add the paste to the pot with the meat and vegetables and stir until you get a nice texture. Stir in the ground sassafras. Serve hot over cooked white rice or noodles.

Serves 4 to 6.

THE GUMBO went over real well. Tommy was at the door when the office workers arrived for lunch and he kept telling the patrons to try the chicken gumbo special. "I have my Pet Mobster from New York cooking for me now." It brought a lot of laughs. And it sold out. The Hearth was a nice restaurant and lounge. The help was attractive and neat. There was Kat, Tommy's old flame. He showed me a picture of the two of them in their prime time, and I'd have to say, Kat was a gorgeous hunk. Another waitress was Denise. She was very nice also. The best and prettiest one of all was a gorgeous young woman named Pamela. She did odd jobs around the restaurant, like bartending and waitressing if she was needed, and I believe she was Tommy's bookkeeper. Pamela was going out with one of Tommy's employee's from the printing business. His name was Max. He was a broad-built, nice-looking man. They eventually got married.

Tom introduced me to the man who owned Howard Uniforms, Charlie Howard. I met his wife, Tracy, also. She was a pretty little blonde girl. Tracy was a beautician. She cut my hair a lot of times and would never charge me. I was her Uncle Joe. Charlie bought some of my books and asked me to autograph them. The people here were really hospitable to me—I liked them all.

It was in the fall of 1997 when I had just gotten off from work and was playing with Giuseppe when my phone rang. I answered, "Hello?" The voice on the other end sounded like a woman from New York. She said, "Joe Dogs? I know that's you by your voice."

I have a very distinctive sounding voice. Everyone always knew it was I on the phone whenever I spoke with them.

"They know where you are," she continued. "You better get the hell out of Birmingham. I'm just trying to warn you, Joe. I found this phone number in my husband's pants pocket. I can be killed if they ever found out that I called you. I'm using my girlfriend's phone, so they won't know."

I was a little frightened over this call and I started to ask her who she was, but I never got the chance, because she came right back in saying, "I can't tell you my name, Joe, because I'm afraid. You met me only once. You were with Tommy Agro. He introduced you to my husband and me. Please don't even try to remember who I am, Joe. I'm doing you a solid. Get the hell away from where you're living," and then she hung up.

I was mesmerized! I couldn't even think. "Was this a prank?" I asked myself. She sounded like a Brooklyn girl. But it couldn't be a prank, because she used that phrase "I'm doing you a solid." They don't talk like that around here. I didn't sleep that night. I was very worried. To top it off my

Yorkie sensed something was wrong, so he barked at every little sound. My .38 was my mate for the evening.

I went to work the next morning looking kind of haggard. Pops and Doris Anne showed concern. I lied and told them I was fine. "I just have a little headache, I'll be all right."

Tommy called ahead and asked me to fix a special salad for a few people that he was bringing over to the restaurant for lunch. "I told them all about you, Joe Dogs. I mentioned that you are my Pet Mobster," he said, cracking himself up. I decided not to tell Tommy about my threatening call.

Panzanella

8 cherry tomatoes, cut in half
1 cucumber, peeled and sliced
1 small red Spanish onion, sliced thin
1 clove garlic, smashed, peeled, and chopped fine
1 cup torn basil leaves
1½ cups extra-virgin olive oil
3 to 4 tablespoons balsamic vinegar
⅓ cup red wine vinegar
Salt and freshly ground black pepper
6 to 8 thick slices Italian bread (crusty baguette preferred),
    torn into bite-size pieces

In a large bowl, put the tomatoes, cucumber, onion, garlic, and basil. Drizzle with the olive oil and then pour in both vinegars: add salt and pepper to taste, and toss well. Refrigerate for one hour. Adjust the seasonings as needed. Add the bread and toss well. If the bread is too dry, add a little more of the condiments and toss.

Serves 6.

IT WAS A WEEK since I got that phone call from that woman, telling me to vacate my place of residence. I wasn't sleeping very well, and I wouldn't answer the phone. I was very quiet at work and Tommy Ray kept asking me if there was anything wrong. "Do you need any money, Joe?" he'd ask. I didn't want to burden him with my problems. If I could only move somewhere within a fifty-mile radius, I'd feel a lot better. Tommy was always slipping me money. A couple hundred here and a couple hundred there. Like every week, he was always handing me something. I just couldn't ask him for more.

Charlie Howard called me on the phone, just after I had talked to F.B.I. Agent Charles Beaudoin out of the New York office. I was telling the agent what had transpired with me and he said he doubted if the government would assist me on a move, but he would try, and then get back to me. Charlie Howard asked me to play golf with him. "After you get off work, we'll play nine holes. I want to talk to you, anyway." I agreed to go after I cooked lunch. Charlie said he would pick me up at the restaurant.

"I got it, Joe! You're my guest—I invited you," Charlie said in the golf shop at the country club where he was a member. What he wanted to talk to me about was a mystery. I was hoping he didn't want me to do anything unlawful. That's been the story of my life, though. Whenever I met someone and they were nice to me the next thing I knew I was always being asked to do them a favor like clipping someone or cracking somebody's head. I hoped it wasn't that.

Charlie and I rode in the same cart and he was a pretty good golfer. We talked sports and kibitzed with each other, although I kept looking all around the area nervously, because of the phone call from that woman. She was in the back of my mind and I couldn't get rid of her warning. I was worried and I think Charlie noticed it.

"What's wrong, Joe? You're not nearly as friendly as you were when you first started working for Tommy. That's why I invited you to play golf with me. Tommy's been worried about the way you're acting. He asked me to see if I could find out anything, and by God, you and I aren't leaving this golf course until I find something out." Charlie was laughing when he made that statement, and he made me loosen up a little and laugh with him.

I told Charlie everything! And I told him I couldn't afford to move any-where. He was very quiet and then finally said, "Well, we have to get you out of there, Joe. You should have said something to Tommy. We're your friends. You are like family to us. I know for a fact that Tommy is crazy about you, and all the people that he introduced you to like you, because they always ask for you. I have this friend who owns a condo in Alabaster. Do you know where that is?"

I answered "Yes."

"If he has it vacant, I'll send a moving van to your house and move you immediately. You can use my wife's brand new furniture that she bought. She was going to put it in storage. She and I split up for a week, but we found out that we can't live without each other and she's back home now. She bought all that damn furniture and don't know what to do with it, so this is perfect. You can use it."

"That's great, Charlie! How much is the rent gonna be? You know I can't afford very much."

"Don't worry about the rent. I'll take care of it for at least a year, maybe longer, and I'm going to give you two hundred a week. No, make that three hundred a week for at least a year or as long as I take care of the rent. Okay now, Joe, you have to promise me you won't tell this to anybody."

I looked at the guy. Was he kidding? He sounds so serious. Why would he want to do this for me? He doesn't even know me, and. . . . Yeah, oh sure, he wants to pay my rent and give me three hundred a week because he likes me. "Sounds kind of fishy to me," I thought.

Charlie persisted, though, and I wondered what it was that he wanted me to do. I was contemplating to myself. I asked Charlie if he was serious, and he said that I would get the three hundred a week starting tomorrow.

"It's Friday, and everyone gets paid on Friday."

"Hey, Charlie, I'm not a homo you know."

Charlie started laughing and said "I don't want anything from you but your friendship, and your promise not to tell anyone about this conversation and what is about to take place."

So I asked "Well, what do you want me to do? I'm not going to whack anyone for you, so why in God's name would you want to do all that for me? I mean, like, sure all you say is beautiful. You'd be saving my life, so to speak, but why?" I still couldn't believe my ears were listening to all these beautiful words.

Charlie looked at me and I swear I must have had tears in my eyes, because this was all too unreal. Here I was worried about having to hurt someone for him or do something illegal, and here he was another godsend. What else could I say to the guy but thank him a couple of hundred times?

Charlie followed through with everything he said. The next day while I was at work he came into the kitchen and slipped me three $100 bills, and told me again that he would never ask me to do anything that he wouldn't do. For the moment, it seemed like an albatross had been lifted from my shoulders again. Charlie had turned out to be a great guy. Between him and Tommy Ray you wouldn't need any other friends. They were two sincere gentlemen. I invited Charlie and his lovely wife over for lunch one day when I was off from work. I made a chicken dish that I thought was very good. Charlie said he was going to invite his brother and his wife if I didn't mind. I told him to bring whomever he wanted.

Chicken in the Oven

8 tablespoons (1 stick) salted butter, melted

¼ cup extra-virgin olive oil

1 cup sherry or dry white wine

4 whole chicken breasts, split

5 Italian sausage links, cut in half (sweet or hot, according to your taste)

6 large white potatoes, peeled and quartered

4 large sweet potatoes, peeled and quartered

2 medium Vidalia (or other sweet) onions, peeled and sliced thick

2 to 3 tablespoons dried oregano

1 (1-pound) package frozen peas

Coarse salt and freshly ground black pepper

In a large, shallow baking pan, place the melted butter and oil, and rub the chicken all over until it's coated. Pour the wine over the chicken. Add the sausages, white potatoes, sweet potatoes, and onions. Sprinkle the oregano over the meat and vegetables. Cover with aluminum foil and bake at 325 to 350 degrees for 60 to 75 minutes. Remove the aluminum foil and spread the peas all over the top. Sprinkle with salt and pepper to taste, and bake uncovered for another 10 to 15 minutes. Adjust the seasoning, and serve immediately.

Serves 4 to 6.

$\mathcal{J}$ WAS HAVING a lot of trouble with Tommy's general manager, Ali. He and I could not get along. He refused to order some of the ingredients I needed to cook the recipes I wanted to make. It's not that the cost was expensive or anything like that. He was just being a jerk. It got so ridiculous—I was in his office one day and he was shouting at me at the top of his lungs about some shallots I had ordered that weren't delivered. I was so frustrated listening to this big mouth jerk from Iraq that out of my frustration, I grabbed him by his tie and pulled him across his desk and held him at bay for a minute or two. I didn't hit him, although I wanted to, the little immigrant bastard. He deserved it. I'm surprised Pops the kitchen cook didn't do it long ago. I knew that I should have never put my hands on the weasel but, to my chagrin, it could not have been helped. Thank God for Charlie Howard. It had been almost a year now, and he was still paying my rent and still giving me the three hundred a week. When this would stop I didn't know. Charlie mentioned one time that if he sold his business he would probably stop sometime after that. So I prayed that he'd never be able to sell it. I guess I was being a little selfish.

The F.B.I. never did assist me on anything that would help me. If it weren't for Charlie Howard I'd have been in terrible shape. If I owed anything to anyone it was these two guys from Birmingham, Alabama, Tommy Ray and Charlie Howard. I just had to be careful and watchful for a while. I didn't want to get myself caught in a jackpot, per se.

November 26, 1997, was a very sad day for me. My mom

passed away. I was terribly upset. I wanted to go to her wake but the F.B.I. office in New York advised me not to go because I was still a hot number in the eyes of the Mafia. "We can't offer you any coverage, and I don't think any agent will offer to put his life on the line to go with you to your mother's wake or funeral. I know how you feel, Mr. Iannuzzi, but it's best that you don't show your face wherever it is that your mother is being presented. I'm sorry I can't offer you any solace, only advice. I'll forward your request to headquarters, and they will follow it through to Washington. By the time I get word back from headquarters, your mother will probably have been buried a month. You know how the government works," the in-house agent said very politely.

I didn't say anything to anyone at work about my mother. I didn't do too well on the job that night. I was drinking while I was working and Tommy didn't like it. I never drank alcohol while I was working, and Tom knew that. But I needed a crutch, and Scotch on the rocks was my crutch this night. Tommy came in the kitchen carrying a steak on a plate saying, "This customer wanted his steak medium rare. Does that look medium rare to you, Joe? This steak is so well done I doubt that my mongrel would eat it. Joe, you're fired. Come to the dining room and sit at my table. I want to talk to you! Doris Anne, you do the cooking tonight" and then he walked out.

I went to the kitchen's bathroom and splashed cold water over my face and neck. I changed my shirt and walked gingerly out to the dining room to Tommy's table and sat down.

"What the hell is wrong with you tonight, Joe? I got three complaints on the food. The customers think that you're not here tonight. One of them saw you staggering, and they told the other people around them that you were wiped out, that's why the food is coming out screwed up. What's wrong?" Tommy demanded.

"Nothing," I said. "I'm just having a bad night. I'm sorry, I didn't do it on purpose." Tommy didn't believe me and ordered me a cocktail, asking me to go to the track with him the next day. I smiled because here he just fired me and we still remained good friends. I had a few drinks and sat there listening to the music. There was a band playing that night and the singer they had was singing a request. The title was "Mama." When she got to the words, "I miss the days when we were together . . ." I started to bawl like a baby. I was sobbing so hard, I was out of control. Tommy came over and took me out of the dining room into his office, and said he didn't know that the job was so important to me.

"If I knew that I wouldn't have fired you. In fact you can have your job back. Go home now and report for work tomorrow."

I laughed so hard that the sides of my body started to hurt. I had to tell him the reason why I was crying.

"Tom—I wasn't crying because I was fired. My mom

passed away this morning. My mother was in hospice when she passed on. I took it for granted that the F.B.I. would come with me to the wake and when they told me not to go and said that they couldn't cover me, everything just added up to disaster for my emotions, especially when the singer started to sing that "Mama" song. I'm sorry I cried like a baby. I couldn't control my emotions."

Tommy said that I should have mentioned it to him, and told me to take the next three days off with pay and then come back to work. I thanked him and left. I went home to prepare a dish that I was going to serve tomorrow for my neighbor and her two girlfriends. They wanted to try a veal dish that I told them about.

Veal Chops Baked en Casserole

4 veal chops, 1-inch thick
Flour for dusting
Salt and freshly ground black pepper
2 to 3 tablespoons butter
3 to 4 tablespoons extra-virgin olive oil
1 pound button mushrooms, sliced
1 large baking potato, peeled, sliced, and sautéed in butter
1 pound asparagus, trimmed and blanched in the microwave
*   for 3 minutes*

Dust the chops with the flour. Salt and pepper the chops and place them in a large frying pan with the butter and half the olive oil, and brown thoroughly on both sides. Grease a covered casserole dish with the remaining oil. Put a layer of mushrooms on the bottom of the casserole, and put the chops on top of the mushrooms. Place the fried potatoes on the chops, and put the remaining mushrooms on top of the potatoes. Top it off with the blanched asparagus. Cover tightly and bake in a hot oven at 400 degrees for 20 to 25 minutes.

Serves 4.

NOTE: This dish can be made with porkchops or chicken.

Macaroons

1 pound whole raw almonds
1½ cups granulated sugar
3 large egg whites
¾ teaspoon almond extract
Juice of ½ lemon
Vegetable oil cooking spray or butter
Flour for dusting baking sheet
Confectioners' sugar

Blanch the almonds in boiling water for 5 minutes. Drain, slip off the skins, and put in a warm to moderate oven for 5 minutes, or until completely dry. In a food processor, chop the almonds with some of the sugar into a powder. Add the rest of the sugar and mix well. Beat the egg whites until stiff. Add the ground almonds, almond extract, and the lemon juice. Blend together with a spoon, gently but thoroughly.

Spray or butter a cookie sheet and sprinkle it with flour. With a tablespoon, drop spoonfuls of batter onto the baking sheet about $1\frac{1}{2}$-inch apart and shape the batter into ovals or whichever shape you desire. Sprinkle the tops with confectioners' sugar and let stand in the refrigerator for 2 to 3 hours. Bake in a 375-degree oven for 5 to 7 minutes, or until lightly brown on top.

Make 22 to 24 cookies.

$\mathscr{I}$T WAS IN THE middle of November, 1998, that I took a trip to Dallas, Texas. I went to see my cousin, Lou, who was living with his fiancée Rhonda. I had made preparations to visit him and have Thanksgiving dinner there. "Maybe I'll let you cook the turkey," he said to me over the phone. So I was on my way and looking forward to seeing him again. Lou was a pilot for some big company, which had a Learjet. My cousin Lou had his own plane, also.

When I arrived at his apartment we went directly to his daughter's house. His daughter Lori was married to a multimillionaire, and they owned a beautiful house. Her husband's name was Frank, and he was a nice-looking Italian guy. My second cousin Lori was a beautiful brown-haired lady, and they had two children. Both were boys. When Lori stood next

to her mother, they complemented each other as they were
look-alike beautiful young women.

I arrived the day before Thanksgiving, so I started to prepare the turkey. I've had turkey a number of ways, and I
found this recipe to taste the best. The moisture that you
receive from the bird is delicious. I prepare the stuffing the
day before but do not stuff the bird until the last minute.

Roast Stuffed Turkey en Papillote

1 extra-large brown paper bag
1 pound (4 sticks) salted butter, softened
1 (18-pound) turkey, washed and patted dry inside the cavity
*   and out*
Freshly ground black pepper to taste
Turkey Stuffing (recipe follows; see Note)
2 to 3 carrots, washed, peeled and cut into 1-inch pieces
1 large onion, skin on, quartered

Butter the paper bag thoroughly inside and out. Make sure
every crevice is covered—this is important. Every square inch
must be covered with butter. Do the same with the bird:
Spread butter all over the inside of the cavity and all over the
outside. Pepper the turkey all over in and out, and pack the
stuffing in the cavity. Put the turkey in the buttered brown
paper bag. Add the carrots and onion pieces around the
turkey. Seal the opening of the bag, so no air can go in or

out of it. Put the bagged turkey in a large roasting pan, in an oven preheated to 300 degrees and bake for 5 hours. Do not open the oven or the bag before the allotted time! When the time is up, let it sit for 10 to 15 minutes before breaking open the paper bag. Let the juices and vegetables fall into the pan that the turkey was baked in. Be very careful not to burn yourself from the steam! Put the turkey on a big platter. Save the drippings for the gravy.

NOTES: If there is any raw stuffing left over after you stuff the turkey, bake that separately.

Also if you want to use a thermometer, stick it in the turkey, but you must seal the bag. This is extremely important. If you read the thermometer before the allotted time you must reseal the bag before continuing cooking.

Serves at least 8.

Turkey Stuffing

Turkeys giblets: gizzard, liver, and neck
6 to 7 celery stalks, chopped fine
2 large white or Vidalia onions, chopped fine
Butter
½ pound Italian sausages
1 large (2-pound) package Pepperidge Farm stuffing
2 Granny Smith apples, peeled, quartered, and cut into small pieces
2 large eggs
Poultry seasoning
Salt and freshly ground black pepper

In a large saucepan, cover the turkey giblets with 3 cups of water. Simmer until soft; strain and set aside the broth. When cool, pull the meat off the neck, chop it with the other giblets, and set aside.

Simmer the celery in the reserved broth until soft. Sauté the onions in butter over moderate heat until translucent. Take the casing off the sausages and crumble the meat into a frying pan. Cook over moderate heat, stirring to break up clumps, until it doesn't look raw anymore.

In a large bowl place the dry stuffing. Add the cooked celery with the stock, the sautéed onions, cooked sausage, apple pieces, chopped giblets, eggs, and poultry seasoning. Add salt and pepper to taste. Mix it all thoroughly. Cover and refrigerate until ready to use.

Make 8 cups.

TURKEY GRAVY

2 to 3 tablespoons flour
Turkey drippings, with the carrots and onion
2 to 3 cups vegetable stock
2 to 3 cups salt and freshly ground black pepper

Place the pan with the turkey drippings on top of the stove over low to moderate heat. Add the flour and stir to make a roux. Cook for at least 5 minutes to make sure flour is cooked thoroughly, stirring constantly so the flour doesn't burn. It should be a tan color. Pour some vegetable stock in the mixture slowly, stirring until you get the right texture, and taste for seasoning. Remember that you used salted butter and you peppered the turkey before baking, so you might not need any seasoning at all. When done, strain into a pot (discard the onion and carrot), and keep warm.

Zucchini and Squash Casserole

1 large turnip
2 or 3 yellow squash
2 or 3 zucchini
1 bunch green onions (scallions)
8 tablespoons (1 stick) butter
¼ cup extra-virgin olive oil
10 to 15 grape tomatoes, cut in half
¾ cup dry white wine
½ cup chopped fresh parsley
1 cup unseasoned bread crumbs
Salt and freshly ground black pepper
1 (15-ounce) jar Cheez Wiz

Peel the turnip. Wash all the vegetables. Cut them in cubes, leaving the skins on the squash and zucchini. Dice the white part of the green onions and slice the green into chive shapes. Melt the butter with the oil in a large sauté pan over moderate heat, and add the vegetables. Sauté until all the vegetables are cooked. Pour in the wine. Add the parsley and most of the bread crumbs, and season with salt and pepper to taste. Toss gently with a slotted spoon for 6 to 8 minutes. Transfer to a shallow casserole dish. Spread the cheese all over the top and sprinkle the rest of the bread crumbs on top of the cheese. Place under a broiler until the cheese is melted and golden.

Serves 6.

Jam Omelet à l'Orange

This is a dessert my grandmother used to make for company on Thanksgiving and Christmas day. This is for two people, so if you are four to six for dinner you must make it two or three times. It's very simple.

3 jumbo eggs
Pinch of salt
¼ teaspoon grated lemon peel
2 tablespoons (¼ stick) butter
3 tablespoons jam of your choice
Confectioners' sugar
1 ounce orange liqueur

Beat together the eggs, salt, and lemon peel. Melt the butter in the frying pan. Pour the egg mixture over into the frying pan. Brown the omelet lightly on both sides. Remove from the pan and spread jam all over one side, then roll up. Place in a flameproof dish. Sprinkle the sugar over the rolled omelet. Pour the liqueur over the omelet and ignite, then serve.

NOTE: This dish is for two people. Slice it in half.

MY STAY WAS very nice in Dallas. I was on my way back to Alabama to pick up Giuseppe at the vet's. There was a guy that I had loaned some money to, and he knew I was coming to Texas so he asked me to stop by where he lived and he'd pay me. I detoured a little on my way back. I called him first and he was pleased that I was coming. When I arrived Louie wasn't at home, but his wife Sandy, was very nice and hospitable. She said that he would be back in an hour or so and she made me feel comfortable and welcome. We small-talked for a couple of hours, and then Louie called and said he was just leaving the area and he would be home as soon as possible. Sandy said that he had a hundred and fifty–mile drive back, so if I wanted to spend the night with them, I was more than welcome. I told her that I could come back another time but she insisted that I stay. "Louie told me to tell you that he has the money that he owes you and he wants you to be here when he arrives." I figured I was in no rush anyway. Sandy and I had lunch together. She prepared a lobster salad and a mint julep. I watched her put it together. She made enough so that when her husband got home he could have some of the salad also.

Lobster Salad

1 (12-ounce) lobster tail, thawed if frozen
Butter
Fresh lemon juice
½ pound tiny shrimp, shelled (salad shrimp)
1½ celery stalks, chopped
1 small onion, chopped fine
¼ cup mayonnaise (Hellmann's preferred)
2 tablespoons ketchup (Heinz preferred)
2 to 3 dashes balsamic vinegar
Salt and freshly ground black pepper
6 to 8 whole lettuce leaves

Cut the lobster tail lengthwise down the middle to butter-fly it. Dot with butter and sprinkle with lemon juice. Broil about 4 inches from the heat for 4 minutes. Let cool with the shell on.

Bring a pot of water to a boil. Add the shrimp. When the water boils again, turn off the heat. Let the shrimp sit in the water until they all turn pink. Drain them well.

Remove and discard the lobster shell after it's cooled. Slice the meat the long way, then cut it into bite-size pieces and place in a large bowl. Add the shrimp, chopped celery, and onion to the lobster. Mix together the mayonnaise and ketchup with the dashes of balsamic vinegar until they blend together. Add salt and pepper to

taste. Pour over the lobster and toss. Adjust seasoning and
serve over the lettuce leaves.

Serves 3.

$\mathcal{L}$OUIE ARRIVED about three hours later. He paid me the
$400 which I had loaned him when he was in Alabama. I
noticed that he took the money from a good size roll. I
decided to spend the night as I had had too many mint juleps.
After Sandy retired, Louie told why it took him so long to get
back here.

"I knew you were coming and I was short of cash so I took
a ride out to the eastern part of the state. I was looking for a
convenience store that didn't have too much traffic. You know,
a store with a gas station. I found one and I went in and
grabbed the guy. I put my piece to his side and told him to
open the register and I wouldn't hurt him. He did like I told
him and I counted the money but there was only two hundred
bucks in there. I told him that it wasn't enough, so he said to
come back in a couple of hours and he would have more
because it starts to get busy with gas. I didn't believe this guy.
He must have thought I was an idiot, to leave and come back.
I brought him in the back room and tied him to a pipe, and
taped his mouth so he couldn't make any sounds. I told him,
"Keep quiet and I won't hurt you." I mean I wasn't gonna hurt
him anyway. I was just scaring him. I went back in the front
and collected all the gas money. A few people paid with credit

cards—you know, with those ATM things. When I thought I had enough I waited until the pumps were empty, then I left. I got almost a grand out of the joint."

"You're nuts" I said to him. "You didn't have to go out and steal the money to pay me. I could have waited. I don't need the money."

"Hey, Joe! You were nice enough to loan it to me. I'm not going to stiff you. You know? I do this four or five times a year. You know!"

"You're a petty thief, Louie. You're going to get caught and then your ass is going to be in jail for a long, long time. You have a beautiful and nice wife and you're going to lose it all, just because you're lazy, you moron. Here, here's the money back. I don't need it and I don't want it! If you get caught, I don't want you saying that you had to do it because you had to pay me. Put it in your pocket or I'll go in your bedroom and wake Sandy up and give it to her. Now I'm adamant! Put the money away!"

"No! Hey, Joe, she doesn't know anything about what I do. She'll leave me if she finds out anything like that. She warned me once, so please don't say anything. Take the money. I owe it to you. I shouldn't have told you what I did."

"That's right. You did wrong by telling me. What did you think—I was going to be impressed by you telling me what you did? You moron. I'm sorry I had all those drinks with you, because now I can't drive in this condition. Louie, I said put the money away. You need it more than me. Take it and go to bed. I'm sleepy and I want to go to sleep. I'll see you in the morning."

Louie showed me my sleeping quarters and I went right off to sleep. I knew I would wake up when the alcohol wore off. I would slip away then. I felt bad that I had to talk to Louie that way, but I had to try to make him see what a mistake he was making of his life. "His poor wife!" I thought as I fell off to sleep.

When I woke up it was four in the morning. That always happens to me when I'm drinking. The alcohol wears off and then I'm wide awake. I dressed quietly and washed up in the bathroom and tried to slip out the door when I felt a hand grab my arm. I wheeled around and it was Sandy. She had her finger to her mouth to signal for me to be quiet. She led me outside onto the porch, where we could talk. In a whisper she said to me, "Joe, I heard everything last night. Here, take this money that he owes you. You drove all the way here for it and you should have it. It's not the money he stole. It's my money. My parents sent me money to leave Louie. They want me to come and stay with them until I get on my feet. So here, take it," she said putting the money in my pocket.

"But honey, I don't want it. You keep it and get the hell away from him. He's bad news. I had no idea he was like this. Here, you keep the dough, and go to your mom as soon as you can," I said to her as I put the money in her blouse opening.

"I'm leaving. Here's my phone number. If you need any help getting out of here, call me and I'll be here in six hours or less," I said as I was getting in my car. I thanked her for the lobster salad and she came running down the steps from the porch and planted a big kiss on my lips. Surprised, I pulled away from the area, knowing that the kiss was for gratitude, and headed toward Birmingham, Alabama.

$\mathscr{W}$HEN I ARRIVED home in Birmingham (home was wherever I resided) I was famished. I had a craving for a peasant Italian dish my grandmother used to make for my grandfather. This recipe is for two people but as hungry as I was I would eat the whole thing, or almost.

Polenta with Sausage

SAUSAGE
½ pound Italian sausages (I prefer hot)
2 tablespoons extra-virgin olive oil
¼ cup finely chopped onion
1 clove garlic, minced
Salt and freshly ground black pepper
1 (14- to 16-ounce) can tomatoes (Cento brand preferred)
1 (10-ounce) can tomato puree

POLENTA
1 tablespoon salt
½ pound (1½ cups) cornmeal
¼ cup freshly grated Parmesan cheese

Prick the sausages and put them in a medium saucepan with ¼ cup water and the oil. Let the water cook out and the sausages brown over medium heat. Add the onion and garlic, and salt and pepper to taste. If using hot sausages, you might not want to use any pepper.) Add the tomatoes and tomato puree and simmer for 45 minutes. About halfway through, start making the polenta.

Boil 1 quart of water. Add the salt, and pour the cornmeal into the boiling water slowly, stirring constantly with a wooden spoon. Continue cooking and stirring until the cornmeal leaves the sides of the pan (approximately 20 minutes). When done, place the cooked cornmeal on a platter and spoon the tomato sauce over, placing the sausages around the sides of the platter. Sprinkle grated cheese over and serve immediately.

Serves 2.

I WAS VERY CAREFUL in Birmingham for a long time. I noticed cars following me, or as I thought so anyway. It was probably paranoia. But I didn't know for sure. I was getting hang-ups on the phone whenever I answered it. I was driving myself nuts. I went out and got three more guns—not from any store, either. I had one in my car, one in my upstairs bedroom in the townhouse I was renting, one in the downstairs area, and the other in my pocket. I stopped going to Tommy's for a while because I was a suitcase. I couldn't relax. I was too edgy to go anywhere. I walked around with a chip on my shoulder and that was wrong. People were nice to me in this area. I couldn't reciprocate to them in the condition I was in, so I stayed away.

I was broke. Charlie had finally stopped paying my rent and giving me the three hundred a week. He sold his business, so I had to get a job doing something. God bless Charlie Howard! He supported me for over a year. What true friends he and Tommy Ray were! I'll never forget them.

I landed a job as a security guard. It was very easy, but the pay was terrible, $5.75 an hour. But, hey, it fed Giuseppe and me. I used to get up at 5 A.M. I would relieve the night guard at seven in the morning. I kind of got used to the hours. I was guarding a milk plant. Then I went on the night shift and it was real slow. I used to play all different types of solitaire. I used to fantasize that I was playing in Las Vegas for a hundred dollars a card. I think they owe me a couple of million. Of course I cheated a little. What a fantasy!

I had to move from the apartment in Alabaster. I couldn't afford it. There was an advertisement in the newspaper to share a house and I looked into it. This young man named David Wright was recently divorced, and he had an enormous house to share. David had two boys and one little girl that the mother took with her, but David had the kids every other weekend. They were well-behaved children, so there was no problem. David turned out to be like a son to me. He was a hard worker and a devoted father to his children. The house was in a wooded area in Alabaster, and there was an enormous security gate. No one could get in the area without alarms going off.

David and I were watching television one night. He had it on A&E channel. I had gone into my bedroom to watch sports on ESPN, when he called me to watch John Gotti in a documentary. You have to know that when I rented the place I didn't tell him who I was, naturally. David didn't know anything about me, but he was about to find out because I was in the same program. I was on the second half. It was called *Mob Rats.* As we were watching the first half about Gotti, David said, "I love to watch all these Mafia programs. I betcha I would've been a good Mafia guy."

He went on and on about that subject so I thought maybe he wouldn't notice me. We were both drinking. I was drinking Scotch and David, beer. The second half came on, and there I was talking and they're showing pictures of me being beaten half to death. A lot of my lifestyle was being splashed on the television screen, and I said to David, "Hey this is pretty good, I think I know that guy."

As David listened to me and the program, he turned to me and said "That guy looks like you, and you know what, he sounds just like you." David was staring at me now. I turned to him and smiled and stuck my hand out and introduced myself, and he was so happy that it was me he did a cartwheel. I explained and told him everything about me and we became real close friends. To this day I call him every once in a while to let him know I'm still alive and kicking. He doesn't know my whereabouts and he never asks; he understands I can't reveal where I am. That's the same with Charlie and

Tommy. I call them occasionally and they're always offering to assist me on anything that I need. Not even my family knows what state I reside in.

I was hungry and so was Dave, so I told him he was in for a treat.

Veal Chops with Marsala Wine

12 tablespoons (1½ sticks) butter, or 1 stick butter and 4
    tablespoons clarified butter
½ pound mushrooms, cleaned and sliced
¼ cup sweet sherry wine
Freshly ground black pepper
Flour for dredging
4 veal chops, 1-inch thick
Salt
Freshly ground white pepper
1 shallot, minced
¼ cup sweet Marsala wine
2 tablespoons Grand Marnier
Juice of ½ lemon

Sauté the mushrooms: Melt 1 stick of butter in a large frying pan. Add the mushrooms, sweet sherry, and black pepper to taste, and cook over a low to moderate flame for 15 to 20 minutes, stirring occasionally. Set aside.

Flour both sides of the chops and season with salt and

white pepper. Melt the remaining butter (or clarified butter) in a large frying pan. Sauté the chops in the butter over a moderate to high flame for 1 minute on each side, and then remove from the pan and set aside. Add the shallot and sauté briefly. Add the Marsala and ignite to burn out the alcohol. Then carefully add the Grand Marnier and ignite. Add the lemon juice. Put in the sautéed mushrooms and stir with a wooden spoon. Put the sautéed veal chops back in the frying pan with the sauce and cook for 4 to 6 minutes, turning them a couple of times. Remove and serve immediately with Asparagus Balsamic.

Serves 4.

Asparagus Balsamic

1 bunch asparagus (approximately 16)
1 clove garlic, minced
1 shallot, minced
1 tablespoon butter
2 to 4 tablespoons extra-virgin olive oil
Juice of ½ lemon
Balsamic vinegar
Salt and freshly ground black pepper

Blanch the asparagus for 3 minutes in the microwave.

Place the blanched asparagus in a sauté pan with garlic,

shallot, butter, and oil. Cook while rolling them over. Add the lemon juice. Continue to cook and then sprinkle balsamic vinegar on top of them. Season with salt and pepper. Serve immediately with the veal chops Marsala.

Serves 4.

I WAS IN MY ninth month on the job as a security guard. The only difference was that I was promoted to captain (I finally made captain! All those years in the Mafia I was just a wiseguy and my salary skyrocketed to $7 an hour. "Wow," I said to myself. "I'm in a different tax bracket now."

Hey, the money wasn't great. But it put food on the table where I was living now with my Yorkshire terrier, and it paid my rent. It felt good, that I was earning my own way, and in three months I would get two weeks vacation with pay. This would be my first vacation with pay, ever. I was trying my best to hold out, but it wasn't easy. I was getting phone calls with hang-ups. I could swear that I was being followed back and forth to work. I'd drive a different route periodically, but the same car was always there. I wasn't even using my car— I was driving David's pickup truck.

One morning, this car was following me. I stopped the pickup in the middle of the road, in a secluded area. I jumped out with my snub-nose .38 in my hand. I was running toward the car, which had a male driver in it, and pointed my gun at the guy's silhouette. The guy ducked and sped past me. I had run to his car about twenty yards beyond me to see who it was stalking me. I knew it wasn't a wiseguy, but it could have been someone keeping tabs on me and trying to set me up for a kill.

I was really concerned. I was worried. I decided it was time to move on. I was happy here but the pressure was getting to me. I started to visualize things. I thought that I was cracking up. I was pissed off. I decided to leave my mark here.

I read the *Birmingham News* daily. There was a reporter on the newspaper who I thought wrote extremely well and made all her exposés interesting. The reporter's name was Carol Robinson. I decided to call her. I did so and she seemed to be interested in my say-so's.

She drove up to the milk plant that I was guarding. A beautiful, petite looking young blonde lady came up to me and introduced herself. I explained to her who I was and the reason for the call. We set up an appointment to meet in a restaurant to have a cocktail on the first interview. I explained to Carol Robinson that this would take a few interviews and she promised me that she would hold the printing until I vacated Birmingham, so my safety wouldn't be in jeopardy.

The meeting went well, and we met one other time. I took her to an upper class restaurant for dinner. Whenever we went somewhere, Carol drew attention. She was well-known in the nicer areas in Birmingham, so it was good being in her company. The final interview was to be at her home, with a photographer and her mother present, along with her beautiful little girl. I cooked them a nice dinner while the cameraman snapped pictures of me in action. We started off with Mario's Mexican Shrimp Cocktail appetizer (page 35). Then we had a salad with blue cheese dressing.

Gourmet Blue Cheese Dressing

1 cup mayonnaise (Hellmann's preferred)
1 cup buttermilk
1 clove garlic, minced
1 to 2 tablespoons fresh lemon juice
Freshly ground black pepper
8 ounces crumbled blue cheese
6 to 8 ounces solid blue cheese, cut into bite-size pieces

Combine the mayonnaise, buttermilk, garlic, lemon juice, and pepper to taste. Mix well with a whisk until blended together. Fold in the blue cheese carefully so as not to break the lumps. Serve immediately or refrigerate until ready to use.

Makes about 6 cups.

Maine Lobster with Crabmeat Dressing

5 to 6 slices fresh rich American white bread (Pepperidge Farm
    preferred)
½ pint (1 cup) heavy cream
2 (6-ounce) cans white lump crabmeat
4 live fresh Maine Lobsters
8 tablespoons (1 stick) butter, melted
Paprika

Remove and discard the bread crusts and tear the bread into
tiny pieces. Put the bread in a bowl and slowly add the
cream, tossing it until you get a paste. Drain the crabmeat,
discarding all the liquid, and add the meat to the bread mixture. Toss lightly until all is mixed well.

Cut the lobsters in half lengthwise almost all the way
through. Open them out and rinse out the liver. Place
them, shell side down, on baking sheets. Put stuffing in the
cavity of the freshly washed lobster. Pour the melted butter
over the stuffing and sprinkle a little paprika over the stuffing for color. Bake in a preheated
350-degree oven for 8 to 10 minutes. Place the lobsters under a
broiler for 1 more minute, to
lightly brown the tops. Serve
immediately with baked potato
and salad.

Serves 4.

Italian Cheese Pie

1½ pounds ricotta cheese
1½ tablespoons flour, plus extra for the pan
¼ cup superfine sugar
Pinch of sea salt
5 egg yolks
Zest of 1 lemon, chopped fine
2 jumbo egg whites, stiffly beaten
Butter for the pan
¼ cup confectioners' sugar
½ teaspoon ground cinnamon
½ teaspoon ground nutmeg

In a large mixing bowl, combine the ricotta cheese, flour, superfine sugar, salt, egg yolks, and lemon zest. Mix together very well, incorporating all ingredients. Fold in the beaten egg whites. Prepare a springform pan by greasing it generously with butter and dusting it with flour. Pour the cheese mixture into the prepared pan and bake in a preheated 375-degree oven for 35 to 40 minutes. Cool on a rack and garnish with confectioners' sugar, cinnamon, and nutmeg. Serve with espresso coffee and sambuca.

$\mathcal{I}$ CALLED CAROL on the phone and told her the date that I was leaving. She promised me that the story would not be printed until one week after I called to say goodbye. She was a beautiful baby doll and she kept her word. I made all the arrangements and moved to Mexico City. I liked Birmingham and it was very sad for me to leave. I'd wind up missing my friends that I made. David started to cry when he found out I was leaving. He was worrying about who was going to cook for him once I left. I told him to follow the recipes in *The Mafia Cookbook*. And then *The Mafia Cookbook* Revised and Expanded was published, so he had a lot of recipes to cook for himself.

ℐT WAS A FEW DAYS later that I packed all my worldly possessions in matching cardboard boxes I retrieved from a liquor store. I was moving away from a place that I learned to love and feel comfortable. My automobile was packed to the hilt. I looked around the house one more time to make sure I didn't leave anything behind. David's two barnyard dogs were lying on the porch looking at me inquisitively. I picked up my pet, Giuseppe, and cradled him in the crook of my arm. I walked over to the two dogs to bid them farewell. My eyes were blurred from the tears building in them. I had a sad feeling in me. I petted and said goodbye to Barney and Bandit. Barney was licking my hand making me feel that he and Bandit were aware that I was leaving and never to return. I started my car and was on my way westbound to Mexico City.

Not long after I arrived, I met this young attractive lady

whom I become a good friend with and she came over to my new apartment and cooked this Mexican dish for me. Her name is Felicia Davis.

Enchiladas

Vegetable oil
2 chopped red or yellow onions
1 red bell pepper, chopped small
1½ pounds ground beef
Garlic salt
Ground cumin
Freshly ground black pepper
½ pound shredded Monterey Jack cheese (2 cups)
½ pound shredded Cheddar cheese (2 cups)
8 ounces (1 cup) cottage cheese
1 package corn tortillas (50 count)
1 (14-ounce) can red enchilada sauce
1 (14-ounce) can chili (no beans)
Lettuce
3 large tomatoes, cored, seeded, cut in tiny pieces
Salsa

Sour cream
Refried beans (optional)
Rice-A-Roni (optional)

Heat a little vegetable oil in a large frying pan. Sauté half the onions and the bell pepper until translucent. Add the ground beef and brown it. Remove all of the fat from the pan. Season the meat with garlic salt, cumin, and black pepper to taste.

Let the meat cool, then mix with the Jack, Cheddar, and cottage cheeses and the remainder of the chopped onion.

Heat the enchilada sauce with the chili.

Heat the corn tortillas until soft. Place a few tablespoons of the filling on a tortilla and roll it up to look like a fat cigar. Place the rolled enchilada in a deep baking pan (ovenproof glass preferred). Repeat this process until all the meat mixture is used. Pour the enchilada-chili sauce over the top.

Bake at 350 degrees for 30 to 40 minutes. Put some chopped lettuce and tomatoes on every enchilada that you eat, along with salsa and sour cream. You could also serve refried beans, and Rice-A-Roni on the side.

Serves 12 to 16.

𝒥 THANKED FELICIA for the recipe and told her we'd have to do it again. She agreed with me and left.

𝒯HE ARTICLE was printed in the Sunday *Birmingham News* and set off a blast that had everyone talking about me. I got someone to mail a copy to the F.B.I. agent and he forwarded it to me at my new location. The article that Carol Robinson printed reads as follows:

JOSEPH "JOE DOGS" IANNUZZI: AFTER MAKING A DEAL WITH THE FBI, THIS FORMER MAFIOSO MOVES FROM CITY TO CITY, COOKING UP A GOOD STORY—AS WELL AS A GOURMET MEAL.

TALES FROM THE MOB

Joe Dogs loves to tell this story: A Catholic priest knelt over him, a Gambino family mobster beaten mercilessly by his peers. Weeping women huddled around the Florida hospital bed as the priest murmured last rites and readied sacramental oil.

Joe Iannuzzi—Joe Dogs, as he was known in The Family for his love of greyhound racing—was broken. His head was battered until its flesh puffed up around his skull, his nose was split open and crushed. His teeth were cracked. An ear dangled. His ribs were broken and his genitals swollen.

Through a fog of pain and prescription drugs, Iannuzzi heard the nurse pronounce him dead.

He bolted upright.

The priest called it answered prayers; the doctor, a miracle.

Joe Dogs called it a chance to even the score. Burning for

revenge, he became one of the government's best weapons against organized crime.

Joseph Iannuzzi shouldn't talk about his days as a made member of one of New York's five infamous crime families. He shouldn't talk about the two years he spent secretly recording Mafia wiseguys or the dozen convictions his testimony won.

But he can't stop.

Since ratting more than a decade ago, Iannuzzi's life has become a succession of low-profile jobs in smaller cities—most recently Birmingham, where he worked for the past nine months as a security guard at one of the city's larger corporations.

Exiled from his past, his family and his failings, Iannuzzi trades on the story to win friends and earn a buck.

"People exploit me, but I'm having fun with it now," Iannuzzi said. "I get a kick. I love the attention."

Iannuzzi is leaving Birmingham for parts unknown.

"Where I'm going now, if I can keep my mouth closed, maybe I'll meet someone I could get close to and have some kind of a relationship with," he said wistfully. "Maybe I'll get away with it. For a week or two."

Not likely. His story is just too good.

Born to be a wiseguy

You can see sadness in Joe Dogs. It's in those once-dark eyes that have faded with age. But there's humor, too. His laugh rumbles through years of cigarettes and Dewar's scotch. He's mobster from head to toe in his mock turtleneck shirts and loafers, dishing out twenties as tips and threats as advice.

"If anybody (expletive) with you or your daughter, don't go to the cops," he says. "You come to me. I know people."

And that accent.

Fuhgedaboudit. To hear him talk, he's Don Corleone.

This image, he contends, was his destiny.

Born in Port Chester, N.Y., in 1931, Iannuzzi was the son of a bookie. Every Saturday, the boy would accompany his father, a former middleweight, on his rounds to collect the bets.

"My father wasn't well-educated. He was almost illiterate. He was a hustler," Iannuzzi said. "He worked as a garbage man, in construction, and in defense when there was a war, but he always had his hands on the bookmaking end. Always."

The mobsters they saw regularly impressed him.

"I saw mob guys coming around, collecting money from him," he said. "I saw how they were treated and respected and everything. They were my idols. . . . I wanted to be just like them."

As a teen, Iannuzzi and his buddies formed a gang called the Night Raiders. They printed up business cards and left them at joints they robbed.

His first pinch, or arrest, came in 1945 when he was 14. Afterward, he hitchhiked to California, where he slept on park benches, painted mailboxes, and stole dogs to collect the rewards.

His career as an L.A. dognapper lasted two months before the cops shipped him home. "I lied about everything, but they finally got my name," he said. "I just broke down and cried."

Several years later, he had fought in Korea, married and divorced. He worked odd jobs in construction or cooking, married twice more and had five children with his second and third wives.

It was during his third marriage that his mob ties strengthened.

"I was looking for an easy buck," he said. "They always had plenty of money, throwing around good tips, so I looked forward to being with them, waiting on them when I was a common man."

He hooked up with bookmakers loosely connected to the Colombo family. Since he was a whiz with numbers, they offered him a gig as a sheetwriter, keeping track of bets and debts.

By the 1960s, he was taking in about $700 a week, tax-free. He worked bookie jobs and ran the grill at a diner. "I became more and more involved."

Living the high life

Joe Dogs still toiled in the minor leagues, but he was turning pro. He left New York in 1968 and headed to West Palm Beach. A recession was on and money was tight, but Iannuzzi took work with a drywall contractor. His unofficial job title was slugger and his duties were to shake down subcontractors. He pocketed $600 to $800 a week.

"Sometimes I was hired out just to provide a little muscle," he said. "I never minded smacking a guy."

Iannuzzi had friends in both the Colombo and Gambino families and did jobs for both.

But around 1970, Joe Dogs had a meeting that changed his life. That's when a pal introduced him to a tough-talking, sharp-dressed mobster from the Gambino crime family.

He was Tommy "T.A." Agro, who ran most of southeast Florida's mob operations as a Gambino soldier.

"My idol. I loved him. Fuhgedaboudit," Iannuzzi said. "Sharp dresser. A lot of money. He acted like a real big-time mobster. We became good friends and close."

Agro immediately staked his claim on Joe Dogs.

"He was my instructor. My mentor. And I learned fast," Iannuzzi said. "I used to walk into a place with a strut on me, fuhgedaboudit. I'd never been in the place before and people thought I owned the (expletive) place."

Iannuzzi was no longer just a sheetwriter. He was a thug and a bully. He beat people and admits to being in the presence of more than one corpse, though he doesn't like to talk about those things. Ask if he's ever killed a guy, and you'll learn a little mob etiquette:

"That's a rude question."

The FBI watched Iannuzzi 24 hours a day. It was no secret. His landlord kicked him out of the apartment when agents told him he was renting to a Mafioso. Iannuzzi moved to a duplex up the street and so did the FBI.

Iannuzzi particularly intrigued West Palm Beach FBI Special Agent Larry Doss.

"When I first came to south Florida, he was about the only organized crime figure around," Doss recalled. "My first assignment was to put Joe in jail."

One morning, Doss and another agent knocked on Iannuzzi's door and identified themselves. The agent and the mobster hit it off. They talked about 45 minutes and Iannuzzi even put away the rifle and three pistols he'd taken out for the occasion.

"One thing you have to understand about the mobster life: We were always talking to feds. Nobody ran from them," Iannuzzi wrote in his book *Joe Dogs, The Life & Crimes of a Mobster*, published in 1993 by Simon & Schuster. "It was kind of an unwritten rule throughout the *Famiglias:* If the Eye approached, tell them what they want to hear, just don't tell them nothing.

"There wasn't a wiseguy worth his button who wasn't polite and blandly accommodating whenever the G (government agents) came around."

Iannuzzi's relationship with the FBI flourished. He tossed them morsels of information, enough to keep them happy but not enough to hurt himself or his buddies. But his relationship with Agro was deteriorating.

Iannuzzi had borrowed $60,000 from Agro and reloaned the money at a higher rate, paying off Agro and keeping the spread. He got behind in his payments because he was having trouble collecting money on his own loans.

That was something he didn't tell the feds, but there was no way to hide it after January 19, 1981.

Agro, along with two of his crew members, was tired of waiting for his money. It was time to make an example out of Joe Dogs.

Agro summoned Iannuzzi to a friend's Singer Island

pizzeria. Iannuzzi went to shake Agro's hand and darkness engulfed him.

"The last thing I remember was Agro himself drawing back his leg and digging his dainty little alligator loafer deep into my ribs," Iannuzzi wrote in his memoirs.

Iannuzzi remembers little about the beating. Doss won't ever forget it. He got to the hospital as soon as he heard.

"He's unconscious. His head looks like a melon. I figured I got this guy killed," the agent said. "His brains are mush."

It took Iannuzzi months to recover. When he did, hate consumed him.

In his mind, there was only one way to exact revenge.

A rat is born

Agro phoned Iannuzzi in the hospital and kept on calling, demanding money. Agro's audacity enraged Iannuzzi. He taped Agro's calls and played them for the FBI.

That's how the feds got what they now call Tape 25— nearly a half hour of Agro spewing about beating up Joe Dogs. There's not one sentence on that tape fit for print, but it would later make a huge impact on a jury. "When we made this tape, we knew we had him" for attempted murder, Doss recalled. "After this tape, I confront Joe. Now he tells me the whole bloody truth. And he wants to get even."

The FBI fronted Iannuzzi money to repay Agro and the two men patched things up, or so the mobsters thought.

Operation Home Run was off and running.

For the next two years, Iannuzzi recorded every mob meeting. He and the feds were inseparable.

Iannuzzi and undercover agent John Bonino, posing as John Marino, set up and ran a mob nightclub. The Gambinos didn't know it was bugged to the rafters. Their sting was so convincing that the Gambinos inducted Bonino as a mobster in the midst of the operation.

"We didn't know where this case was going," Doss said. "It had a life of its own."

The case lived until September 1982, when the government decided to end Operation Home Run. It wasn't long after that Iannuzzi's cover was blown. An overly ambitious FBI agent in New York cornered Agro and tried to bait him into becoming an informant by telling him of Iannuzzi's cooperation.

"It goes through the whole Mafia within a matter of hours that Joe is a rat," Doss said.

During the next 10 years, Iannuzzi testified in 12 trials.

The FBI paid him $3,800 a month and moved him from city to city, state to state.

"He was good. The proof of the pudding is do you convict" Doss said. "For all of Joe's shortcomings, his strength was the truth. One thing Joe never did was lie."

Iannuzzi's testimony sent more than a dozen people to prison. In 1986, Agro pleaded guilty to loan-sharking, extortion and attempted murder and was sentenced to 20 years in the Florida State Penitentiary. In 1987 he was granted a medical parole to die at home, which he did that June from brain cancer.

Among the others Iannuzzi sent away were Colombo boss Carmine "The Snake" Persico; Gambino capo Andrew "Fat

Andy" Ruggiano, released from prison last year and a contender to take over the Gambino Family; Riviera Beach, Fla., Police Chief William Darden; Agro sidekick Bobby "Skinny Bobby" DeSimone, whose brother Tommy was played by Joe Pesci in the movie *Goodfellas;* and a list of other Gambino and Colombo capos, crew members, and sluggers.

"Some nights, after sitting in that witness stand putting my old pals away, I went back to my room and cried," Iannuzzi said in his book. "I got into the whole thing for one reason. I wanted revenge on Tommy Agro."

Life on the run

Iannuzzi got his revenge, but at a price.

"New towns, new places, new faces, and new lies I had to tell," he says. Under an assumed name, Iannuzzi moved around the Southeast and even opened a small bagel shop in Florida. It went under during one of the longer trials. Iannuzzi begged to get into the witness protection program, but the process was lengthy.

In 1992, in southern Florida, his past caught up. The daughter of a man he put away spotted him at a convenience store. Not long after, as he drove along Interstate 75, a dark sedan passed him. He saw two arms emerge from the front right and rear window with guns. Shots rang out.

"My life flashed before my eyes. The good times. The bad times," he said. "I kept seeing my children's faces, their cries."

Iannuzzi ducked and slammed on the brakes. Bullets pelted his car and bounced off the pavement.

"They almost got me," he said.

Days later, he was in the witness protection program.

"I stayed in hotel after hotel for about six months. Different cities, different states," he said. "I wound up in Memphis. I stayed there for a year and a half."

Iannuzzi is not a fan of the protection program.

"You go to get a job; you got no references, and they're not going to lie for you," he said. "They don't help you get references for an apartment. You have to go out and muscle it yourself."

Despite the program's requirement of anonymity, Iannuzzi also began muscling his way to public attention.

He sold his autobiography for $250,000 to Simon & Schuster and in 1993 published his *Mafia Cookbook.* He was offered a spot on the David Letterman show to promote the compendium of high-cholesterol recipes and gory war stories.

He says he told the feds he was going to do the show, and no one told him fuhgedaboudit. Iannuzzi made it to the set, but his segment was canceled at the last minute.

Nonetheless, a New York newspaper caught wind of the story.

Cookbook sales soared. Joe Dogs was booted out of the witness protection program. The government gave Iannuzzi $7,500 and a kiss-off.

He moved to Charlotte, N.C., on his own and stayed six months.

"I would walk my dog. Go to a bar. Meet friends. I had money, you know. Money from my book," he said. "Then I got tired of that. I heard about Birmingham having a racetrack."

Iannuzzi settled in a Hoover apartment in January 1994,

but despite proximity to greyhounds and betting windows, life was no better. "I was in a shell for $2\frac{1}{2}$ years," he said. "Nobody knew who I was."

For a guy like Joe, that's real punishment.

"I was very depressed," he said. "My phone bills were astronomical. I was reaching out for anybody to talk to."

He called people he hadn't talked to in years.

"They were glad to hear from me, but, you know, I made my own bed. I hadda sleep in it," he said. "And then I got to be like a pain . . . to them. They never said that, but I know."

Iannuzzi decided to leave Birmingham about 1997. He had started to make friends and, because he thought he'd soon be gone, he let a few of them in on his secret. And then, Iannuzzi agreed to talk to an over-the-mountain civic club about his adventures and his books.

"From then on, everybody started to know who I was," he said. "It was my own fault really."

Iannuzzi sometimes hires out to his new friends, or their friends, cooking one of his lavish multicourse dinners for small parties of some of Birmingham's wealthier residents. The shtick goes like this: While Iannuzzi's in the kitchen, the host shows a videotape of Joe Dogs' interviews with A&E or the Discovery Channel's recent special, *The Rise and Fall of The Mafia*. Then, he emerges from the kitchen and the delighted guests find out their chef is a real, live former mobster.

"People get off on it," he said. "You know, they say, 'Hey Joe Dogs, I got somebody I want you to whack' or 'Hey Joe Dogs, I wish you'd been there . . . '

"I'm glad I wasn't there because they'd have to see Joe Dogs ain't what he used to be."

Habits remain. At a recent dinner at Ruth's Chris Steak House, Iannuzzi gave the maitre'd $20, and then the hostess another $10 for escorting him about 10 feet to his table.

"What I miss about what happened before was the glamour," he said. "I don't miss smacking people around or taking advantage of people."

Iannuzzi replays those times in his mind.

"At night I'm alone with nothing to do but think about my past. All the bad things I did. All the good times I had."

Iannuzzi believes the threat to him persists, though more mob snitches are going public with their stories. He always has a gun in his front right pocket. In his right rear pocket is a worn leather glove with sand sewn into the knuckles.

"When I wake up in the morning, I look around. I first look to see where my dog is," he said.

Doss agreed that Joe Dogs is still, and will always be, in grave danger.

"Joe needs to have a lot of luck and hope that he's not in the wrong place at the wrong time," the agent said. "If that ever happens, he's a dead man."

Moving on

Birmingham has been home to Joe Dogs longer than any other city in the past two decades and his stint as a security guard is the longest he's ever held a legitimate job.

"And now I have to leave. I'm very sad about that," Iannuzzi said. "I get up at 5:30 a.m. to be at this job. Please. When I was mobster, I used to come home at 5:30 a.m."

Iannuzzi knows he needs to keep his mouth shut. He's got to stop telling the story.

"It's so hard for me to do it. I'm my own worst enemy, sure," he said. "That's why I gotta move again."

And he's got to make people like him all over again. That's his life.

"I try to buy my friendship with a lot of people," he said. "Some people resent it. Some people take advantage of it.

"But I want to be liked. It's a nice feeling to be liked."

Joe Dogs packed up his life in a few cardboard boxes last week. He didn't say where he was going because he wants to shoot for anonymity this time.

But asked what he told his supervisor when he gave notice, he hesitated.

"I told him who I was," Joe Dogs reluctantly admitted. "Then I went to my car and got him two cookbooks out of my trunk."

ONCE I WAS SETTLED in Mexico City, I went out for a view of the city. There was a warm breeze that probably came from the Gulf of Mexico. "It's beautiful here," I thought. I went into a bar and restaurant, and had a late lunch, with a couple of Scotches. It was about three in the afternoon. I usually don't have any alcohol before 6 or 7 P.M. But I was in a new area and the time changes made me want a drink. I became friendly with the owner there. His name Leo Paso, a 100 percent Mexican. He had beautiful Latina women working as waitresses in the place. I naturally tried to become friendly with some of them. My success was with Katrina, the lovely hostess. Katrina had straight, long, black hair that fell to her lower back, and extremely dark, beautiful eyes. When I complimented her on her hair, she said it was hard to keep it looking the way it does. She told me she brushed it twice daily, approximately fifty strokes each time without fail, so it would look beautiful.

"Women have to work hard to keep our hair looking good. You men don't have to do nothing but wash, dry. And run a brush or comb through it. You guys are fortunate," she said.

After a few weeks of patronizing the place, I got to know the help a little better. Katrina invited me to her hacienda for lunch. She wanted me to try a zucchini dish, Mexican-style.

Chicken Zucchini

2 tablespoons vegetable oil
1 pound boneless and skinless chicken breast, cut into cubes
1 clove garlic, minced
1/4 cup chopped red or green bell pepper
1/4 cup chopped onion
3 medium zucchini, trimmed and diced
2 or more chicken bouillon cubes, crushed
Dash of ground cumin
Pepper
Salt (optional)
1 tablespoon minced fresh cilantro

In the oil in a large frying pan, brown the chicken and garlic together. Add the chopped pepper and onion and cook until translucent. Add the zucchini, chicken bouillon, and cumin. Season with pepper and salt to taste (or add more chicken bouillon). Simmer 15 to 20 minutes, stirring occasionally, until the vegetables are done. Just before serving, add the cilantro. Serve with white or Spanish rice, black beans, and tortillas.

Serves 4.

NOTE: You can substitute pork for the chicken, but omit the onions.

$\mathscr{K}$ATRINA AND I became close. She wanted to get married. Me? Fuhgedaboudit! I just wanted to be her boyfriend and take care of my pet. Even though Katrina was a lovely lady, with all the right ingredients, I just wasn't capable of marriage again. I told her maybe some day. But not anytime soon. Who knows what tomorrow brings? Tell me and I'll make a fortune.

The night that Katrina proposed to me she introduced me to a Mexican dish that made me almost accept her hand in matrimony. Almost, but not quite. Although it really was delicious and very spicy.

Chiles Rellenos (*Mexican Stuffed Chilies*)

8 green poblano chiles

STUFFING
Vegetable oil
1 small potato, diced very small
1 pound ground beef
1 package taco spice mix
Flour

BATTER
5 jumbo eggs, separated and yolks lightly beaten
Dash of salt
Vegetable oil for frying

SAUCE
1 large sweet onion, sliced into rings
2 tablespoons cooking oil
4 large tomatoes, peeled, seeded, and chopped fine
Salt and pepper
Shredded Monterey Jack or Cheddar cheese, or crumbled farmer's cheese

Char the peppers in a dry heavy skillet over medium-high heat, turning them constantly, about 5 minutes, until they are toasted. Place them in a plastic or brown paper bag for 15 minutes. Remove them from the bag and pull off the thin layer of skin. Cut a small hole in the bottoms of the peppers and remove the seeds. Try to leave the stem intact. Set aside.

In a large frying pan, cook the potato in a little oil until golden. Add the beef and taco mix and cook according to the package directions. Let cool a little. Insert about an eighth of the stuffing into each pepper. (Use a small spoon, pastry bag, or a plastic bag with a corner clipped off.) Dust the stuffed chilies with flour and set aside.

Make a stiff meringue with the egg whites and salt. Gently fold in the yolks. One at a time, dip the stuffed chilies carefully into the batter and immediately put into hot oil in a large frying pan. Let fry for about 5 minutes, or until golden, turning them so the other side cooks as well. Remove from the pan and place on paper towels to drain excess oil. Repeat the process until all 8 stuffed chilies are fried. Keep in a warm oven until ready to serve.

Sauté the sliced onion in the oil until translucent. Add the tomatoes and salt and pepper to taste, and cook on moderate heat until the sauce turns orange.

Place one or two stuffed chilies on a plate, and pour about ¼ cup of the tomato sauce on top. Sprinkle Monterey Jack, Cheddar, or farmer cheese over it. Serve with white rice, beans, guacamole, and sour cream. A margarita with this dinner complements the dish.

Serves 4 to 8.

NOTE: You can substitute sweet red or yellow bell peppers for the poblano chiles to make this dish milder.

WHEN I FINALLY got the article that Carol Robinson wrote, I read it and called a few people in Birmingham. I wanted to know what the reaction was. David told me that all his friends were flabbergasted. I called a couple of female friends and they were surprised. One of them said not to call her anymore, as she was afraid for her life because of the brief affiliation she had with me. Another said that she was thrilled to know me and that I was a brave person to do what I did. I had mixed reactions from the friends that I had made. A lot of them wanted me to come back to Birmingham and a few begged me to stay away.

Me? Hey, I figured I'd keep writing books. Why not? I finally got a computer, and I'm wearing out two fingers down to the nubs. By typing, that is. So I bid y'all farewell, until my next book.

Ciao

Introduction

$\mathscr{C}$OOKING HAS BEEN a big part of my life. I remember when I was a little boy. I always watched how my mother cooked pancakes and oatmeal. But whenever she boiled eggs I would run and hide under the bed. I hated the taste of soft-boiled eggs. She would scream at me from the top of her lungs, "Junior, eat your eggs, or you'll never grow!" Somehow I didn't believe her. Then again I figured if she was telling me the truth I could always be a jockey. They were small but tough. So I chanced it every morning. No eggs cooked! I'd sit down and eat. When I saw the eggs unshelled, I'd be under the bed in a flash.

When I said I wouldn't eat soft-boiled eggs, I meant it. That is, until I felt the leather from my father's belt on my soft little white butt. I figured the belt tasted and felt worse than the eggs. The sting lasted longer! So I became a connoisseur of soft-boiled eggs.

When I was twelve years old, my mother entered me in a cooking contest with fourteen other tiny chefs, all under thirteen. Everyone cooked some sort of eggs. Some of the others, mostly little young ladies, cooked scrambled, fried, or poached eggs. I cooked soft-boiled eggs. That's how it all started.

As I grew older in my teens, I worked in different restaurants such as hamburger joints, hot dog stands, and pizza parlors. When I enlisted in the army in 1948, I tried to get in the mess hall as a cook and the chef told me he would teach me how to cook. He handed me a potato peeler and gave me an artistic lesson on how to become a chef in the army. Through the Korean War and out of the service, I wanted to become a chef, or at least a top-notch cook. So I ventured in the food line. I worked at a number of different restaurants. I was good. I became a saucier and I owed much of my learning to an executive chef named Edmund Muller.

So it was my cooking that really made the mob guys put their arm around me and let me come into their good graces. Through my cooking I was able to hang around them and travel with them to different places, and I was the elected chief cook and bottle washer. I was "cooking on the lam" so to speak. Once in a while the mob guys would take me along with them, to help them with something illegal. But not too often. I was mostly out shopping for the groceries for that evening meal.

Now, we were in a lot of small cities and you would imagine that it would be difficult to find the right ingredients for this cookbook. Wrong! I must tell you that I never had that problem anywhere. Take, for instance, Birmingham, Alabama.

You would think that only if you were making soul food you hit the right state. No, sir! I went into a store called Bruno's Supermarket, and went to the canned vegetable area and purchased Cento brand canned tomatoes—my favorite brand. They also had fresh basil there, so I was in like Flynn. There were many other grocery stores there that had good brands of whatever product I needed.

I of course am no longer with the Mob, because they beat me half to death for overcooking their fettuccine. So I have to move a lot. I know that the grocery stores all over the country carry the ingredients that are needed in this cookbook, without any problem at all. All you have to do is shop. Of course, after you purchase this cookbook. So, if you buy, enjoy. If you don't buy the book, borrow your neighbor's.

Ciao, and *buon appetito*

PS: I finished 15th in that egg cooking contest that my mother entered me in.

*H*ERE ARE a couple of more recipes without stories.

Shrimp Fra Diavolo

⅓ cup extra-virgin olive oil
2 cloves garlic, minced
1 shallot, chopped fine
2 pounds jumbo shrimp, cleaned, deveined, and butterflied
2 (16-ounce) cans stewed tomatoes
6 dried chile peppers, soaked in olive oil
Salt and freshly ground black pepper
1 pound angel hair pasta or linguine
Freshly grated Parmesan cheese

In a large sauté pan, heat the olive oil over medium heat. Add the garlic and shallot. Cook until tender, being careful not to burn the garlic. Put the shrimp in the pan and toss them until they are pink. Crush the stewed tomatoes and add them in the pan. Cook on medium heat for 2 minutes. Stir, and reduce the heat to low. Add the chile peppers and simmer 4 to 6 minutes allowing the flavors to blend into one another. Season with salt and freshly ground pepper.

Meanwhile, cook the pasta al dente, according to the package. Drain.

Serve the shrimp over the pasta, sprinkled with Parmesan cheese, with a loaf of crusty Italian bread and a dry red Burgundy wine.

Serves 4 to 6.

Molly's Chocolate Cake

This is a hand-me-down old family recipe that my mother gave me when she was alive. She told me that her mother gave it to her.

> $^2\!/_3$ cup vegetable oil
> 5 squares (5 ounces) unsweetened chocolate
> $2^1\!/_4$ cups sugar
> $1^1\!/_4$ cups boiling water
> 1 teaspoon vanilla
> $2^1\!/_4$ cups sifted flour
> $^1\!/_2$ cup buttermilk
> 3 large eggs
> 1 (6-ounce) package chocolate chips
>
> ICING (OPTIONAL)
> 1 (1-pound) box confectioners' sugar
> $^2\!/_3$ cup chopped nuts
> 1 tablespoon vanilla
> 8 tablespoons (1 stick) butter
> $^1\!/_4$ cup cocoa
> $^1\!/_3$ cup milk

Melt the oil and chocolate squares together in a large pot. Once melted, stir, and add the sugar, water, vanilla, flour, buttermilk, and eggs. Beat together to form a nice blended batter. If the mixture feels too loose, add a little more flour.

If it's too dry, add another egg or a little more buttermilk. When the batter has the right feel, fold in the package of chocolate chips. Bake in a greased 9-inch round pan at 325 degrees for 25 to 35 minutes.

If you'd like an icing on the cake, mix together the confectioners' sugar, nuts, and vanilla until well blended. Set aside. Bring the butter, cocoa, and milk to a boil. Mix together with the sugar mixture, and spread over the cooled cake.

Great Northern Bean Soup

4 to 5 cups dried Great Northern beans
1 (16-ounce) can Italian tomatoes (Cento brand preferred)
2 onions, peeled and quartered
3 or 4 cloves garlic, minced
Enough stock to cover the beans by 1 inch or more (chicken
*   stock preferred)*
Salt and freshly ground black pepper

Place the beans in a 2 to 3 gallon pot. Cover the beans with stock by approximately 1 inch. Let them sit overnight, covered. The beans will swell slightly. Add more stock to cover the beans by approximately ¼ inch. Put on to boil over moderate heat. Once the stock starts to boil, lower the flame and add the tomatoes, onions, and garlic. Simmer covered until the beans are tender, stirring the soup occasionally and making sure not to let it burn or stick to the bottom of the pot. Season as you go along with salt and freshly ground pepper to taste. Add more chicken stock as you go along, if it gets too dry. When soup is done, let it cool slightly and then puree it in a food processor. If you use a blender, be careful not to burn yourself. You'll have to do this in batches.

Reheat the soup gently and serve hot with a healthy spoonful of Lemon Butter in each bowl.

NOTE: You can use water instead of chicken stock, but then add a ham bone or a couple pieces of ham for flavor. Take the bone or ham out before you puree the soup. Dice the meat, and add it back when you reheat the soup.

Lemon Butter

5 to 6 tablespoons butter, softened
½ cup chopped fresh parsley
5 to 6 tablespoons extra-virgin olive oil
Juice of 2 lemons
2 cloves garlic, minced

Whisk together all the ingredients until blended.

Post Script: Giuseppe

*I*F I HAD TO DO this life all over again knowing what I know now about the Witness Protection Program, I would tell them to "flake off." I never once felt safe or appreciated for my efforts against organized crime. All I did was make a bunch of attorneys and F.B.I. agents prominent in their careers. The agents I didn't mind; those so-called marshals? Fuhgedaboudit. They wouldn't give you the time of day. The taste I have in my mouth for the Witness Protection Program is unprintable. The program needs a lot of work and changes. They need people like Abraham Lincoln in their organization. If you're a killer and you rat for the government, they treat you a lot better than if you're a cooperating witness.

My pet was attacked by a wild deer that almost killed him. It was an eight-point buck that came down with his hoofs trying to kill my nine-pound Yorkshire terrier. I lived in an area where the deer were plentiful. There would be forty to fifty deer on the property every day, lounging around like pets. My Yorkie's eye was damaged so bad that he became blind. The veterinarian recommended that I put him down. I refused. I nursed him with the help of the veterinarian, back to where he could get around in the house and go to the bathroom outdoors. His other eye was almost deteriorated and badly in need of surgery which I couldn't afford. Everyone around me told me it wasn't worth it keeping my dog alive to see for a year or so. I didn't agree. How can you base your love for an animal on dollars and cents? I tried desperately almost everywhere to see if I could borrow money for my pet's surgery, to no avail. I was determined to keep Giuseppe alive as long as God would make him prevail. (For those who are concerned, God punished that deer severely.)

A month later I moved back to Vestavia, Alabama, a small suburb on the outskirts of Birmingham. My friend Tommy Ray helped me financially on this move. His niece, Stacy, lived in the apartment that I was going to rent. She was going to Europe for a couple of years so she left me a bunch of furniture. She was a godsend, as I had nothing. Stacy had the electric and water turned on in my name. My friend Matt Veal's wife Felicia gave me a bed to sleep on. Matt gave me a dresser. All my friends chipped in to make me feel and be comfortable. My state of depression was gone.

At Tommy's bar that night, I told him of my pet's misfortune with the deer, and that his other eye was almost gone. A veterinarian, Dr. McGee, overheard what I was telling Tommy and he asked me to bring my pet in to see him in the morning. Dr. McGee had been Giuseppe's vet when I previously lived in Birmingham. I did as he requested and Dr. McGee examined Giuseppe thoroughly and refused payment, but recommended an examination by an eye surgeon. The surgeon wanted $1,300 for the surgery on the one eye that was saveable. Her examination that day was an additional $150. I told her I would mail her a check. The surgeon agreed. I knew that the mailing the check statement was the second biggest lie in the world, but what was I to do?

Tommy called me at my residence and wanted to know what the surgeon said, and I told him. I told him that Giuseppe would have to keep banging into walls until he figured out where he was. Although Tommy didn't see me as we were talking, my eyes were shedding a stream of tears after what he then said: "Come to the bar now and pick up my check for $1,300. I'm going to see that that little fella spends the rest of his life as comfortable as he can be. Come on now and have a drink and don't worry about the money. It's on me!"

After gaining my composure I went to Tommy's Up Top, his bar. Tommy also gave me the $150 to pay for the initial visit. Birmingham was where I belonged.

I stayed in Birmingham for a year, but started to feel uncomfortable again as everyone knew who I was. I felt that it was time for me to leave. I've lived all over this continent and I'm at a place now where no one knows me.

Giuseppe, my beloved pet and best friend, got a terrible kidney infection. He didn't eat or drink any liquids for three days. He was lethargic and moaned. The local vet told me it was time. I pleaded with him to save him a little longer. The veterinarian told me I was being selfish. "The poor animal is suffering, Joe. Let's let him rest."

I agreed with the doctor. But I wanted to spend one more night with my little boy. I took him home. It was five o'clock in the afternoon. I lay Giuseppe on my bed and I cradled him in my arms. The veterinarian had injected fluids into him because he was dehydrated. We lay together all night, me singing to him and crying and my pet wetting the bed. I didn't care. He was my life.

At seven the next morning, I drove tearfully to the vet's office and left my beloved pet with the nurse. I have a large photograph of him on my dresser where I kneel daily and say a prayer for him. Giuseppe was almost eighteen years old.

ACKNOWLEDGMENTS

First of all I want to thank my beautiful daughter Sheryl for helping me tremendously, and for letting me put some of her delicious recipes in this book.

Special thanks to Julie Hawkins for being my friend at a time when I really needed one. Your e-mails cracked me up. I miss them.

To my good friend, retired F.B.I. agent Charlie Beaudoin, thank you for the clam sauce recipe that you got from your aunt. It's delicious.

I don't want to forget to mention pretty Felicia from Albertson's. You remind me so much of my daughter Sheryl when she was your age. Thank you for being my friend.

Also to my good friend, Bob, and his extremely lovely beautiful wife Emily. Thanks for sharing your expertise and jump-starting me on learning to operate this computer, and also for all the potato vodka martinis. I'd like to make mention of Jenny, Bob and Emily's daughter. Jenny, you're the epitome of beauty.

I'd like to thank my cousin Rhonda and her boyfriend Lou Salfi for all the free cocktails in their bars. I wouldn't have paid for them anyway.

Thanks also Anthony and Tonya Colagrecco for their encouragement on the writing of this book, and the recipe that Tonya gave me. Their little girls Bianca and Sophia are beautiful, smart, and precious. Also thank you Grace Padula for that wonderful recipe. God bless you.

Thank you, Carol Bowie, for your input, and the answer to most of the idiotic questions that I would ask.

I'd like to thank all of my friends in Birmingham: Tommy Ray and his lovely wife Carolyn, Charlie Howard and his beautiful girlfriend Tracy. My pal David Wright and his good-looking sweetheart Katrina. Also thanks to some of the people I worked with at Tommy's Up Top: Donna, Denise, Kat, and Doris Anne the chef. Special thanks to veterinarian Dr. McGee for his care of my pet, Giuseppe.

I would be remiss if I didn't mention what my eyes see as the loveliest and sweetest looking young lady in Birmingham, Felicia Veal, the wife of my close friend, Matt Veal. Thank you, pal, for all your invitations to your and Felicia's home.

And to the sexy beautiful-looking Leah Hearing, thank you for coming into my life!

And much thanks to Carol Robinson, top reporter for the *Birmingham News* and Linda Stafford, also from the *News*, for their help in getting me permission for the completion of this book.

Also I must mention Charla, and her sexy girlfriend Leslie. You're two degenerate gamblers. (Only kidding, ladies.)

And fuhgedaboudit! I have one more. To my friend Michael Korda. Thank you, thank you, and thank you, for giving me the opportunity to continue on with my writing. You'll always be my friend. God bless you.

Ciao

Joe Dogs

About the Author

Joseph "Joe Dogs" Iannuzzi was a mobster with the Gambino crime family before teaming up with a deep cover F.B.I. informant and appearing as a star witness at eleven major mob trials. He entered the Witness Protection Program after testifying and is the author of *Joe Dogs: The Life and Crimes of a Mobster, The Mafia Cookbook,* and *The Mafia Cookbook—Revised and Expanded.*